Living Truth

Living Truth

Jean Klein

Edited by Emma Edwards

▶◀ Third Millennium Publications
St. Peter Port • London • Santa Barbara

Living Truth

ISBN No. 1-877769-24-X
Library of Congress Catalog Card No. 94-061608

Interior design and production by Janet Andrews
Albion Studio, San Rafael, CA

Cover: Fragment, Royal Sarcophagus, 1500 B.C., Palace of Knossos, Courtesy of the Museum of Herakleion, Crete

MASTER OF ADVAITA VEDANTA in the tradition of Ramana Maharshi and Atmananda Krishna Menon, Jean Klein spent several years in India going deeply into the subjects of Advaita and Yoga. He returned to the West in 1960 and has been teaching regularly in Europe and, more recently, in the United States. He has published many books on non-dualism.

In the late 1980s he was invited to give seminars in the Santa Cruz Mountains of California. In this isolated, peaceful mountain setting, a small group of students gathered with their life questions. The conversations of the 1988 seminar were transcribed and printed as a pamphlet entitled *Mount Madonna Dialogues*, but it was felt that the contents of all of the seminars were rich and rewarding enough to be gathered into a more substantial publication. This book is the result.

Recognition

My deepest gratitude to Emma who has made the teaching accessible and the book readable. She has kept intact the purity of the teaching which remains alive only in the absence of the I-image.

Jean Klein

Acknowledgments

Without the help of Janet Andrews, Mary Dresser, Stephen Follmer, Pat and Barbara Patterson, Worth Summers, Charles Surface, Richard Miller and many other generous souls, this book would not exist. Our heartfelt thanks.

Table of Contents

Mt. Madonna
July 1987
—

July 12

I want to ask a question about what you said once about listening and welcoming. When I first heard you talk about this it struck me like a revelation. This condition seemed a most appropriate way to be, to always be, but I found that it also showed me that I seemed to be constructed in exactly the opposite way. In other words, I find that I never really welcome, I never really listen. I assume a posture of defense, of not listening to myself, not being open. What can you say that would give me an indication as to how it would be possible to be in the welcoming, since it is really the opposite of how I always am?

Very often when you listen to something, you emphasize the object. There is still an action; there is still eccentric energy, I would say. In welcoming, you emphasize the welcoming. That means in welcoming you are completely open, open to the perception. In welcoming you are waiting, completely directionless. You live freely without any representation, without psychological memory. Your real nature is welcoming.

When you come to the understanding that there is nothing to achieve, nothing to obtain—that all knowledge is a going away from what you are looking for—then there is a spontaneous giving up. You do not give up, it gives itself up. Then there is welcoming and another way of listening where the listening and the welcoming are open to themselves. It refers to Itself. Welcoming, listening, is an impersonal state where there is no place to be somebody, to be a person. That is why in welcoming you are spontaneously excited. Excited is not really the word—you are completely expanded. The moment the person comes in the play, you are contracted, fixed to the body.

Do you live in a state of emptiness? I mean, when you are in meditation or even walking down the road, are you always in a state of emptiness?

Emptiness is not a state; I correct you, it is a non-state.

I'm curious to know whether, when thoughts spring up out of that emptiness, do they go on a quarter of your time, or three-quarters of your time, and if they do, how can you keep your mind still all the time like that? Aren't you wanting to think about things?

I never think.

You never think. When you answer a question, are you not thinking?

No. I hear the question in silence, and the answer comes out of silence.

Don't you yearn for something? Isn't there a yearning, a magnet that is pulling you or bringing thoughts into you that makes you want to think? I'm trying to understand, because it used to be that I did not think; I used to space out when I was a child and I would just be nowhere. I would repeat a phrase over and over again or I would have a picture in my mind and would go through a whole picture and repeat the picture again and again. So I would not think. To get out of that, I worked to think, and now it is like a

4

process—always wanting to go on. I always have to have my intellect going on.

What is the motive of this intentional thinking?

Knowledge, excitement, discovery.

But in the end what do you want really? Happiness? Joy? Peace?

Yes, joy; exciting joy.

So you think in order to find happiness. And have you found it?

Oh, yes.

So you are happy?

Yes, I am.

Well, marvelous!

I have states of spontaneous ecstasy where it...these time periods of incredible ecstasy, just joy and excitement and wonder...there have been time periods in my life, and then they go away and are not there any more....

You go away.

You mean, I go away?

Yes, be aware of these moments when you go away.

When I go away from the ecstasy, or when the ecstasy is not there any more?

You go away from your real self.

Oh, I see. So, you are saying that the joining of the self is the ecstasy?

You go away from your real self. Be aware in the moment when you go away. In happiness and in joy you cannot say, "I'm happy," "I'm in joy"—it is not possible. When you think, "I'm happy," you objectify it, make it a state. Where there is happiness, nobody is happy, nothing is happy. There is only happiness.

You are still involved in calculative thinking, looking for a result, an experience. Real thinking is when you go away from thinking. When you look away from thinking, that is real thinking. All real thinking starts free from any thought. Real thinking comes out of silence. You may have a certain fore-feeling of what you are looking for.

I get really confused with the terms: what is thinking and what is not.

What you understand by thinking starts with thinking. That is intentional thinking, superficial thinking, surface thinking. That is not thinking at all.

Just an exercise.

Yes. Real thinking starts from the unknown, from silence. This thinking has a completely other way of flowing, I would say. There is never assertion, there is never domination, never manipulation. This thinking is constantly in a state of "I don't know." The background of real thinking is "I don't know."

So is the excitement that comes out of the "I don't know" the excitement of the non-state?

Yes. You are completely open to the unknown. In any case, what you are looking for you cannot know. All that you know is representation. When you say "I know," you represent it. Thinking is in representation, but your totality—what you are fundamentally—can never be thought. You can only *be* it.

This is my first seminar with you and I would appreciate knowing something about your life, your background, your path, how you came to where you are. I have heard that you don't tell, so I decided to ask myself.

Do you know your motive for coming here? Don't be too quick; you have time. You do not have to give an immediate answer, because a quick answer may come from the mind. Be careful. Look, really, at what is your motive to come here.

I think I know; my motive is to find peace of mind.

Perfect. That means you have not found it; you are looking for it.

Yes. Someone mentioned your name, and I decided right away to come here, without thinking.

Yes. It is an adventure, a risk.

Right. Well, I'm a risk-taker.

Yes, you are an adventurer. I like adventurers. Will you pay the price for what you are looking for? Any price? Are you willing to live free from the person? Do you see that the person is the biggest price?

Does that mean that you are not willing to share your past?

You can only share with me what you are fundamentally. That we have in common. That is not a relationship between personality and personality. When you pay the price of giving up the personality, then you can really share with me what we have in common. There is really nothing to ask. You would like a biography.

Can you further explain about the giving up of the personality that you just mentioned? Is that like giving up the name, fame, shape or whatever that one has?

I would say that you cannot give up the personality, because you give up the personality still from the personality. The personality can never give itself up. It is only through understanding that the personality dissolves. You must absolutely understand that the personality in itself does not exist. In certain circumstances it acts as a vehicle, as a tool. So you must not identify yourself with your personality. Use the personality how and when the situation asks for it. Then you will have a real personality, not a constipated personality, a fixed personality. See that the personality that you have taken to be yourself is a collection of experiences and second-hand beliefs. At least eighty percent of your beliefs are second hand; there is very little personal experience in it. So your personality is not original, flexible, creative; it is stuck. When you see it, you will not use it any more; you give it up, or rather, it gives up itself. You use it when life asks for it. Of course, the personality is a very useful tool, but the moment you identify yourself with it, it is a very heavy luggage to carry.

If the personality is not real, then who is it who pays the price?

The mind sees that what you call the personality is only memory. When the body wakes up in the morning, where is the personality? You need to think of it. The personality is thought. When I say you must pay the price, it means that the mind must see its limits, its restriction. The mind cannot think beyond the personality because the mind has so successfully identified itself with the personality. What you are fundamentally, you cannot think. It is the personality with which you identify which covers your real nature. The moment the personality gives up, the idea of being somebody gives up, then you will knowingly be your freedom. You will live your emptiness, your totality.

So it is the personality who pays the price.

The personality has its own place in your life, a very important place.

Why is it, then, so hard for us to pay the price?

I think it is a very high price, because we are so deeply rooted in the representation to be somebody. Our surroundings, our society, take us for somebody. If we take ourselves as somebody we can only see somebodies around us. So, what is the relationship between human beings? It is only the relationship between somebodies. And this somebody is a fraction—is rooted in insecurity, fear, the anxiety to be recognized, to be loved, and so on. And so the relationship between human beings is only asking, demanding. When you live in your real nature there is no asking, there is only giving. Because there is fullness.

There are a lot of techniques around for realization. Do they work?

You should see that the real relationship with our surroundings is in non-relationship—when we are constantly open. Otherwise, it is only a relationship within clichés. It is a relationship between furniture. It is important, in daily life, that you see that your fixed ideas make furniture of the people around you. And when you really see, stop. Stop, and see how the seeing acts on you, the impact it makes in you. That is important. Just seeing is already something, but you must follow it to the end. How does the seeing act on you? Only there is the transformation, the revolution. Without this bi-polar seeing, no revolution is possible, because this transformation does not go through the mind. It is an instantaneous understanding when all the facts have been seen.

What makes you do what you do with this understanding and with your life? What motivates you to do this?

You are only this understanding; you are not more than this. In this understanding you will see what is life and what is death. Then, you live in happiness and make your surroundings happy. What more would you want?

I wondered about your specific choices to play this role. With this understanding, why do you do this?

There is nobody to do it.

There is nobody else to do it.

Nobody does it.

Is it a passion for this?

No. Nobody does it. There is not a doer. It is you who superimpose a doer. There is no doer.

In the life in which your body moves and you sit here and you teach, why do you do it this way?

My body likes to sit in this way, but there is nobody who moves.

Can I ask this question in another way so that I will get a more specific answer?

If the question does not come from books or from curiosity, ask and I will answer. Please.

I love your understanding, and I would like to know what it feels like to be you—in that understanding. I do not know you; we have never met, and as you were teaching me today....

I do not teach you...no, no, no, I do not teach. You do not understand. There is not a teacher.

As you were allowing me to be in your presence today, I was aware of the fact that you did not know me and it was not an intimate connection or a personally loving connection which I still think is real in the world even in emptiness, and I wondered what it was that led you to be sharing this way with a stranger.

It is only love. There are no others. There are no strangers.

Can you speak about your passion? Is there such a thing?

11

My passion? What do you mean by passion?

I think that passion is the underlying force, the life force. I think that it is at the very heart of existence. I think it is not understandable, I think it is not explainable, I think it is the energy of life itself.

When you look for truth, when you look for beauty, when you look for peace, then you look with passion—to take your formulation. Yes, that is passion, because this passion comes from truth and from beauty itself. And your passion? You love beauty? You love love? I know, you are a fortunate woman.

Oh yes, very fortunate, very blessed.

[Another questioner] You were talking about giving up the personality. Does giving up the personality include giving up the importance of things that are meaningful to you and make you happy? Let us say you are a musician, a composer, and you would like to find someone who supports you, so you would be able to compose and get a deep satisfaction from composing. Do you have to give that up when you give up the personality?

I would say, see that you are more than your personality. Why live in restriction? In other words, see that you identify yourself as a personality—you go around as a personality, you look at things around you, beauty, truth, with this personality; that means you live in restriction. See the real value of what you call the personality. Do not identify yourself with it any more than you identify with your house or your car. Then you are completely free. Nothing is wrong with the personality, absolutely nothing.

But do you have to give up that need for satisfaction from things

12

*that are important to the personality to get to the stage where you
do not identify yourself with your personality, or are they simultaneously compatible?*

See only that when you identify yourself with your personality
you live in restriction. What is the use of the personality? Face
your daily life free from restriction. See that all that is perceived, all that is thinkable is an expression of life, an extension of life. When you really understand that all existence is
an expression of life and that the only mission of these
expressions is to jubilate, to admire life, then you use your
personality for thankfulness throughout your life; and then
you use it in the right way.

*Well, you see the thing that really struck a deep chord is the price
that you are talking about; what price?*

From the point of view of the mind, from the personality, it
is a very high price. I think you would rather give up your
bank account than your personality. Letting go of the personality is a very high price.

*But when you give up your personality, might the price include
your bank account?*

Absolutely. The personality asks for tremendous security.
When you are free from the person there is no more striving
and you know your real needs. When you really deeply
understand that the personality is an hallucination, it is a very
little price to pay.

Is the personality the same thing as the ego?

When you do not think it, where is the ego?

13

What personality does one use if one does not use the memory personality?

When you are free from memory, there is no more choice. There is choiceless living. In this choiceless living all your intelligence and creativity are at your disposal.

The openness that you mentioned tonight—is that your true nature, or is it in the realm of becoming?

When you live in your openness, then the openness refers itself to itself. That is beingness.

That beingness is something beyond everyday consciousness, would you say?

Beyond.

Beingness is something more basic than normal consciousness.

It depends how you take the word "consciousness." When the attention is sustained, it unfolds in intelligence, in sensitivity; it becomes consciousness, it becomes alertness, it becomes timeless awareness. It is presence.

You mentioned a moment ago that there is no teacher, yet you have also spoken of the necessity for a guru. I have come here to be with your teaching in the hopes that it will enliven me into my consciousness and my beingness. Would you speak to that?

We are here to clarify the mind. The mind should know the perspective that something is that is not thinkable. In other words, the mind should know its limits. When this occurs, there is a spontaneous, natural stopping of mind function and we find ourselves in a completely new dimension. In this new dimension there is nobody; there is only love. So, first let us be clear about what is meant by a guru-teacher. If there is a teacher, it supposes a possible pupil-disciple. But when somebody takes himself for a teacher, for a guru, he lives in dependency, in insecurity. And when you take yourself for a student, a disciple, you also live in insecurity. As long as we take ourselves for somebody, we are in insecurity. In the new dimension we spoke of, where the mind gives up all representation, there is no disciple and no teacher. So I give you no hold to take me for a teacher, and I do not take you for a disciple. In this non-relation there is magic. There, you can really speak of magic.

A few moments ago, you delineated a few different steps. There is attention, sustained attention, and various stepping stones along to enlightenment, and yet there seems to be also just an instantaneous awakening, and I'm wondering if the clarification of the mind or the sustained attention—what role that plays in connection to the instantaneous awakening.

The mind must become informed. When the mind is informed there is a natural giving-up. In this natural giving-up, where there is nobody to give up, there is an instantaneous apperceiving of one's real nature.

It seems that what you are describing is not an intellectual process, but an awareness of just beingness.

It is a form of maturity in life which brings you to certain questions. It is only a mind that has attained this maturity that can ask questions. And one must have many questions; one must live with one's questions, not try to understand the question with the already known. That means we must live with the questions in our emptiness. When we live so with our questions there comes a kind of discrimination, discernment. From all those questions we come to the fundamental original question: Who am I? This question, Who am I?, only comes when you have inquired in all possible directions. Only when you have explored all the directions do you come to the mature state of asking Who am I? In this question, Who am I?, a mature mind says, "I don't know." It is only in this "I don't know" that there is anything knowable, perceivable. For the "I don't know" is not a blank state, the real "I don't know" refers to itself and there the question is the answer. That is an instantaneous apperception of ourself. That is our timelessness. When we have explored all the directions, there is a natural giving-up. And then what you give up—what gives up—has a completely new significance.

When you say exploring all the directions, do you actually mean to try all the directions that you think are going to give you happiness?

I would say, yes.

So if you think that you should have your own private jet, do you think you should try to get that?

Because you are an intelligent man, you will eventually see, in inquiring and exploring, that the moment you got what you wanted there was a moment of absence of all energy, of all striving, of all becoming. In that moment when your desire was attained, you felt completely free. When you really live these moments, they are completely causeless. It is a moment of desirelessness where you are in your peace, free from all need and projection. But you ignore the beauty and autonomy of those moments by attributing to them a cause: a new woman, a new car. And when the desireless moment passes you are again looking for a new cause, a new direction. You have gone in many directions and found moments of desirelessness, of happiness, and as you immediately attributed these non-states to a cause, you wasted their power, and the so-called cause, a few days later, is completely without any taste.

This vicious circle will eventually bring you to the conclusion that you can never find what you call peace and joy on the phenomenal level. Then you really ask for life.

Is that why it seems as if the times I have known the kind of freedom and happiness of which you speak seem to come after I have felt a deep despair in which I have almost given up—nothing seems to work—then suddenly I feel free of it all. Is that what you are speaking of?

Yes, you give up all the directions. And then there comes a stop.

Can I give up yoga?

Ask yourself what brought you to do yoga and what brings you to give it up. You do not need to give up your singing, your piano playing, your golf. You do not need to give them up. Why give them up?

The other day in a yoga session you talked of a timeless moment and my mind merely went: Well, this is a timeless moment, dot, dot, dot; then I realized that it was a tasteless moment—there was no taste. Is that what you are talking about?

You can never think of a timeless moment, because thinking is in time. You can become completely attuned to the moment; then you cannot think and you are really present. You can

17

never think of presence—when you think of it, it is already past. You can only *be* presence.

How can I, in asking this question, right now, experience that attunement?

The moment you ask a real question, you are free from the answer and you are free from the question. You are automatically in a "don't know" where your mind is completely free from representations. There is just waiting and being open. This openness is reflexive, referring immediately to your whole intelligence, to your whole sensitivity. It does not look at life from here in your head, from here in your body. In this waiting there is the answer. You can never have the answer on the level of formulation. You will have these timeless moments between two thoughts and between two perceptions. You will see that between two perceptions or two thoughts there is a nothingness. There is wholeness, there is life. This, you will have often in daily life. At first you will be in these moments before a thought and after a thought, before a perception and after a perception. In the end you will also have this presence during a perception, during action. Then it is like the juggler you saw when you were little and your father took you to the circus. He was juggling twelve balls with only two hands—very difficult. Every ball came down at the right time to the left and the right hand. How did he do it? You noticed that he was not identified, implicated, in the play. He was behind his doing.

When you live your totality you will be behind all your actions. All will come and go in this background, consciousness. Thoughts will arise and die, action will appear and disappear in consciousness. This consciousness is your presence, your real nature. It is the only continuity. Be attuned only to what is constant in you.

Thank you for listening.

July 13

I wonder if I might pursue the question that I asked last night. I asked about the relation between the teacher and the student, and you said that there is no teacher and there is no student. And it seemed to me that if there is a teacher and a student then there is a whole ground for expectations and desires to arise. I think that I understood what you meant, because if there is a teacher and disciple it destroys the relationship. And yet I am still aware that in all the great traditions there is the talk of the role of the teacher, and you have spoken of and used the word "guru" in past talks.

You must first see that in reality there is nothing to teach. Then the problem disappears. One can teach knowledge but one can never teach what one fundamentally is. One can only teach what one is not. On this phenomenal plane, on the phenomenal level between teacher and disciple, we can only say what we are not. So, when the teacher says that you are not this or that, it belongs to the mind. But we can only say what we are not because we are. So, saying what we are not comes out of what we are. So, this saying has a certain perfume, a certain background, a certain taste. When you follow with your mind the understanding of what you are not, it will lead you to its source as a shadow leads to its substance, and there is a moment of apperception of reality. In the understanding that all that is, we are not, there is a moment when there is no more reference to the already known; there is just silence. But in this silence the person has no security and so the mind comes in and begins again.

When you have lived freely, lived knowingly the not-known, you will be solicited in daily life. It is like a recall of this non-state. You will first have it when an activity is completely accomplished, between two thoughts, two perceptions, and then there comes a moment when you have it in action. That is important. But coming back, one can only teach what one is not. In this way, the mind is informed, the mind sees that it has a limited role to play.

Pedagogically speaking, in order to say what we are not, we must first know the nature of what we are not: body, senses and mind. We cannot simply say, "I am not my body," because this saying is superficial. But when you come to really know your body and you say, "I am not my body," it is different.

Yesterday, we were talking about experiencing different things so we would find out that they are not the answer and we would drop the personality. I want to ask another related question and that is what psychologists have defined as the basic human needs: love, security, protection, etc. And obviously all of us have certain lacks in some of those areas: love, for instance, security, etc. Should these lacks be fulfilled or satisfied before we can drop the personality? Is that sort of a direct route, or can you bypass these needs, or are they going to come up later on?

Your body may have certain requirements, but don't you know that you are not the body? The body appears in your awareness and its likes and dislikes in a certain way go on.

So it is not that fundamental a need, then? Like if your mother did not love you when you were two years old, you do not have to find another mother before you lose your need?

20

No. No. But you should never give up anything, because giving something up voluntarily causes conflict.

To what are you referring—giving up what?

The body may have certain needs, why give them up? That is a calculation, there is no spontaneity in it.

Well, if you satisfy it, it certainly is not the answer. If you do not satisfy it, will it hinder the answer?

Likes and dislikes are compensations. When you have found your real nature there are no more compensations; there may remain natural needs, that is true, but there are never compensations. There is a kind of establishment of hierarchy, I would say.

There are times when seemingly causelessly I experience a feeling of despair or fear, a sinking feeling which does not seem related to an event. I think you have said that one should accept and find a good feeling and allow the despair to be encompassed by the good feeling. But I discover that I cannot find a good feeling at those times. I can find the despair and the rest is neutral. I cannot find a place to begin to work with.

When we speak of accepting, it is not a fatalistic accepting, but an accepting with the view to know what you accept. So, accepting means not to interfere with your perception. Simply remain completely alert to what you accept. Then one day you will find yourself in the accepting state itself. You can never localize this accepting stance. Accepting is not outside or inside. It is not a concept. It is a state of openness. Because, in accepting, you live in fundamental certitude that all may come to you. It comes to you; you can never take it, you never grasp it. All you can do in your life is, I would say, to wish it, and even the word wish is too powerful. Be completely open to whatever happens to you. That is non-volitional living. There is a very deep wisdom in not grasping, not asking, only waiting.

So there is nothing more to do with this feeling than with other feelings—just be all of them?

You have been approaching my suggestions from the psychological view. The fear is located very often in the abdominal region. Face the physical location and in locating it in an actual part of the body, you will be able to deal with it in a concrete way.

You spoke about the energy body. Are there different bodies, or is it one flow?

You are born with a certain energy capital. You can augment this capital, it is true. You can organize, you can reorchestrate your capital. You can administrate it wisely or unwisely, but you are born with a certain capital and it is important that you come to know it and administrate it well. But you can only become a good administrator when you are completely detached, when your ego is not involved. When you administrate with psychological distance, you use your capital in the right way—all your capital, your energy, your intelligence, your sensitivity, your money, and so on.

You have said so often in your lectures and your books how important it is for us to see that we cannot find what we seek in objects. We come to the point, you said, where we see they do not give us what they promise. Now, in my life experience this is true. In each experience I wait, in an almost passive way, for the

22

disappointment. Is there a way that I could see, in a sudden convincing way, that I will always be disappointed in objects, without having to go through the whole series of calamities?

When you emphasize the object, then you are constantly in its possession. But when you really see that the object cannot give you what you are looking for, in this moment you have a forefeeling of what you are and there is no more dispersion and there is orientation. When you are oriented, all your life is reorchestrated. But as you cannot willingly give up your desired objects, you must really see that when the desired object is attained, in this moment there is nobody and no cause of this moment. There is absolute joy without cause. That means accepting that the fundamental joy in you *is* you. It is important not only to see it, but to see how this seeing acts on you.

Yes, now the problem is, as you know, that the mind chases the next desire and the next one very quickly.

Yes, it is not enough simply to see, but take note how the seeing acts on you, how it affects your organism. This will bring you to maturity. When you question your life, when you explore your life, you will see that there is a dispersion of energy in hoping, wishful thinking, daydreaming, and so on. With this observation comes discrimination. This discrimination does not come from the mind; it comes from the facts of the situation itself. The only meaning the object has is to point to the ultimate subject. When you use the object in the right way, you come to the understanding that every object is sacred. An object becomes sacred when you see really that its homeground is in ultimate awareness. I would say that an object not only points to, but is used to glorify the ultimate. That is why we have art, beauty.

It is not very often in our life that an object is not produced from another object, that it really comes out of silence. When an object appears in silence it does not belong to the mind. It belongs to our totality.

You are aware of your actions and reactions and your resistance; it is important that you see your resistance, otherwise you remain in the chain of resistance, of reaction. The moment you see it you are out of the process, out of the chain of reactions, and then when you see it you stand in a certain way outside the process. When you really stand outside the process I would say this out-standing refers to itself; you feel yourself free.

In those moments when everything drops away and there is no more tension, no more thought, there is just stillness and silence and this infinite sense of well-being and no more questions, is there anything one can do in that moment to deepen it? It's like what happened today when I went for a walk and the one thought that arose was that I don't want to leave this place; I don't want to go away from here.

The appearance—the enlightenment, if you like this word—is instantaneous, is constantly new; it affects your phenomenal being, that is sure, and in your phenomenal being there may be many changes which belong to space and time. The uneducated mind objectifies it.

The mind is very clever. In a certain way it is against life, because the mind knows that there is no place for its psychological play in living truth. Of course it functions when necessary in daily living, but eighty percent of its activity is to maintain the personality; and when you do not use the person any more, because then there is no more psychological memory, the energy dispersed in psychological activity is reoriented, brought back to stillness. There is functional memory, of course, but psychological memory has no longer a reason to exist.

Do you think it is necessary to cut back on daily activities to be more available to that deeper silence or stillness?

You will be invited. You can never provoke the invitation. Stillness is not in time or space and does not need time and space to be. Stillness is the background of all activity. When you no longer act from the personal point of view you will automatically find your activities are economical, efficient. You cannot change by will. Only a right understanding, a clear perspective can bring change.

July 14

The starting point of all activities is more or less localized in our heads. But the moment we are invited by our original stillness to be the stillness, then we should go away from this localization. Otherwise, we remain enclosed in the battlefield. When you are invited to be still, consciously relax your optic nerves. In our sense activities the eyes play a big role and the optic nerves are generally in tension. All the energy employed in seeing is more or less in intention. So, when you feel tension in the eyes you should, with the help of your optic nerves, let the localization go through the left and right brain away from the eye area so that it feels as if the eyes are localized at the base of the brain. Then you are out of the battlefield. You will feel that all the energy which comes up is more or less localized in the cervical region, very precisely at the seventh vertebra. You should enjoy for a certain moment this localization. Then you may be invited by your deep relaxation to go to the heart. Perhaps the heart is the last door, for there, there is no more outgoing or ingoing.

Have you any questions?

Concerning that energy that I feel sometimes coming very strongly through me, years ago you told me, "Welcome the visitor and let him visit you without manipulation." When I work and I feel that energy coming through my heart and my hands, I have no problem. It is really a healing energy and I feel I am totally flowing with life and am at peace and it is a celebration. When I am not working and I feel that spring of strong energy coming, instead of feeling it through the heart and the hands, I feel it coming to the head. It sometimes makes me feel tremendously aggressive, I do not feel that element of love, I feel personal. If I try to hold it back I feel it becoming nervousness. It is much better now, but I still have it at times and I do not want to manipulate it. However, I still see it being transformed into nervousness. Could you help me? Is it simply through observation once more, seeing the personal element that I have to let go?

The word "observation" is very heavy. I would say, welcome your nervousness. In the moment when it comes up, have the feeling of your whole body. You cannot immediately feel the whole body, but there is a kind of gathering of all the parts of your body. Welcome the energy, welcome the nervousness. You will see how difficult it is to welcome, because the welcoming position is completely free from any direction. The moment you feel that you are localized, concentrated, that the energy is fractional, sit or lie down, and let your body be an object of your observation. In observation you are free from all manipulation, all direction, all thought. Then the energy expands and integrates in your totality, instead of being focussed in one place.

There is an organic memory of the body in its natural, relaxed, energetic state. Memory is not localized only in the brain. Our cells contain memory, an organic memory where you feel your body whole, completely orchestrated with the energy. You must become acquainted with it.

Also, come to know yourself in the mirror of society, when you are with people in many different situations. The moment you feel a reaction, face it.

And accept without judging.

Yes. Then your reaction goes away immediately, because there is no fixation, no localization possible. The moment your attention opens, unfolds itself, it becomes intelligence, it envelops all your sensitivity. Then your seeing is no longer fractional, your seeing is global.

So I should not try to control the energy.

There is not a controller, because the controller has the same nature as the controlled. It is the subject which maintains the object. But when the subject is no longer relative, when it becomes the ultimate subject, then there is no more fuel for the object, and there is a fusion between the observer and the observed. It is the controller which maintains the object.

You may, it is true, through the controller, find a more comfortable place for your object. You can make the object peaceful through many techniques. But it is still a lion. You may give some food to the lion, caress it and appease it, but still the lion is there.

You said, "when the subject becomes the ultimate subject...." Could you elaborate on that a little?

An object exists because there is a subject, and the subject exists because there is an object. What we generally call the subject is an object too, because we can observe it, we know the nature of this subject—its fear, anxiety, expectations, and so on. Suppose there is fear in your body. The moment you, as the subject, try to calm the fear or give some justification for it, you contribute to it. That is why the controller belongs to the controlled. But when the observer relaxes in pure observing, he loses his qualification as a subject and vanishes in the observing. And as the object no longer has an accomplice for maintaining its fear, it dissolves. Then there is no longer an observer and something observed.

You can find many appeasements for your fear. You can practice relaxation, you can become a rich man, have a big house, a nice car—all these kinds of things make your fear temporarily peaceful—but the fear is still there.

When I think about who I am and who we all are and what we are doing here, I think: I am here to become this attentive awareness, I am here to become myself. And we are here to commune, to mingle with one another, to feel our oneness with one another. I wonder what part there might be for celebration, for singing, for dancing, and if that would be contradictory to your work. I wonder if you think about humanity and what humanity means, if you care or if that is an illusion. I also wonder about this teacher-student relationship that is, in a sense, enforced by this kind of exchange, particularly when we do not have more play between us. Not that we cannot play when you are not here, but there is no organization to play, to celebrate together. I would like to understand where you are in relation to these things.

In celebration we use the expressions of life, and the expressions of life can have many forms—music, dancing, singing, painting, play, all kinds of forms which point to beauty. But you know that the real music is after the music, the real dance is after the dance. So that any celebration vanishes in joy and you do not *need* to go through the celebration form. You do not need to dance or sing. You can go immediately to your homeground.

And there is another way of celebrating, even when you are not expressing a special form of art. It is a togetherness where there is no asking, no demanding, there is only being together. Sometimes you see people who live in harmony together. There is nothing left to say and they are comfortable in silence, because the togetherness never changes. It may be dressed differently, but it is always the same. In science when they say, "We have found something new," there is nothing new: It is always the old, dressed another way. There are couples living together for whom there is nothing more to say. And it is so intense, this living together.

But is it all right if we sing together or dance together when we work with you?

Oh absolutely!

I wanted to ask you more about becoming the ultimate subject and observing the subject and object. I find that if I have a feeling of compassion about what I am observing in myself or something else, it works better. I do not know if I am fooling myself, making that up and creating something that is just in my mind.

Accepting is compassion. When you hear or see beauty, it brings you immediately back to the ultimate. When you see how you function, the way you think and act, you must not be stuck to the seeing. It is not enough just to see and to hear. You must see where the seeing automatically brings you: to your peaceful, natural, vacant state. What is important is the result of the seeing. As I said yesterday, look how it acts on you. See to which state the seeing brings you. Spontaneously, activities stop; you are in the light of totality.

I want to question more about action. My circumstances have been such that I have been able to sit on the sidelines, so to speak, for the last few months. The more I taste the silence and space, the more there is a reluctance to act. It is almost as if action were a dark tunnel I do not want to go into any more. My job (I work at home) entails writing about things that have no meaning: management theories. These concepts of dreamland...it is almost visceral, you know. I feel I have been in a cesspool. I do not want to go swimming there any more. Sometimes I think I would rather die than go in there again.

It is not important what you do. It is the inner state in which you do it. Next time you will not emphasize the thing done, the object, you will naturally come back to the doing. You will be in your natural stand and feel yourself, establish yourself in this nothingness. Here, nothing is represented, but there is presence, there is fullness.

You were speaking about the optic nerve, and how that can help us to release tension. I would like you to speak more on that.

First you will see that your eye activities are constantly in action. Of all the sense faculties, sight is the most grasping. So, relax your eye activity. First, relax the eye cavity. You may ask how to relax it. One way is to imagine you have very big sunglasses on. In front of each eye there is a big, big sunglass. Then expand the cavity to this size of the sunglass. You will see that a kind of relaxation comes.

Go back to the eye itself. Try to imagine that the eye is falling completely out of its cavity. At a certain point of relaxation you will feel that all the eccentric energy becomes concentric, comes back, and then you consciously cross the brain on either side. In this way, you have the impression that both of your eyes join in your neck.

Take note how this activity acts on you. You will immediately feel that your brain, which is constantly contracting and expanding like a sponge, becomes relaxed. You will notice that the pulsation moves from a contracted to an expanded form. Though there is still movement, it is moving in the

32

expanded form. For a certain while you should localize yourself here. Then you must have the impression that, with the help of your tactile sensation, you expand behind you to cover the wall behind you. You will find that not only your neck but your back covers the whole wall.

Then you may automatically be taken to localize yourself in your heart, not the physical heart, but the heart of all hearts. It is still a localization, but it is the last door which brings you neither inside nor outside, to the ultimate nowhere.

The moment you remain enclosed in the battlefield in your brain, there is fighting.

You said that when you are expanded behind "you may be taken in the heart." Why "may," and is this heart felt as an expansion from in front or from behind?

It is felt in front. I cannot give you a guarantee. It depends on many things.

I have experienced a state where, instead of the observation being on specific objects, it is over all objects. The same is true of sounds. Does that experience relate to what you are saying?

You will see that when you look at specific things, your looking is concentrated. You need to learn to look as a painter looks. The painter never concentrates on the object itself. The painter looks at an object in connection with other objects, because, knowingly or unknowingly, the painter knows that an object in itself has no autonomous reality. It has its reality through the other objects around. One object reflects another. So an artist has a relaxed looking, seeing how the object acts and how light gives life to objects. When you come to the right relaxed looking, there is another state where there is still seeing but nothing is seen.

As long as you have eyes, there is seeing, but nothing specific need be seen. As long as you have ears, there is hearing, but nothing specific is heard. In daily life, in meditation, there is no withdrawal of the senses.

In certain texts they speak of withdrawing the senses. That is a wrong expression. It is not a withdrawal. The senses come to their natural non-directed state. There is seeing but nothing is seen. There is presence without restriction.

I do this sometimes when I am driving a car, but it is a little scary. I let the body drive the car. I am no longer in control, but I think I am a better driver because I see everything. Is this what you mean?

Yes. In this moment, there is no thinking.

It is automatic.

If you like, automatic. There is no thinking, especially when you drive in places where the traffic is very dense and you have no time to think. There is only seeing, pure seeing, pure perception. There is only function. There is not a functioner.

You said yesterday in response to my question about a plastic flower and a real flower that from the ultimate perspective there is only beauty. But I am wondering. It seems that there is a difference in objects.

That is true. When you see a real flower and an artificial flower, it depends on the capacity of seeing. When you see an artificial flower there is still an absence of life that you find in a real flower.

I am interested to know what the relationship is between con-

*sciousness and evolution. Did Neanderthal man have sages? Or
is awakened consciousness a recent phenomenon that is tied in
somehow with the evolution of the species?*

There is only consciousness. You cannot apply evolution to
consciousness. Consciousness *is*. But the expression of consciousness is without end, is a basket without a bot-
tom...though the form may change. What does it mean,
evolution? It is only a category of the mind. When the proto-
type of a thing has changed, it is no longer here. It is finished.
It is only the mind that "changes" it from one thing to another
thing. Because in reality all appears and disappears in consciousness and there is no independent phenomenal continuity. But that brings us too far in the problem of evolution.
Consciousness has nothing to do with evolution.

Are you saying evolution is a thing of the mind?

Yes, the mind.

*There are many expressions of consciousness, and that other
question was whether, in order for consciousness to know itself,
are specific forms required?*

It depends on how you take the word "consciousness." When
I speak of consciousness, I speak of pure consciousness. But
very often there is some confusion. When I think of pure
consciousness, I think of pure awareness. I take the formulation to which I am accustomed. For me *all* is consciousness.
There is pure consciousness, and then there may be functional
consciousness. Functional consciousness is when there is the
presence of an object. Generally, one speaks of awareness and
consciousness. These terms are very often confused.

Monkeys do not meditate. Do monkeys meditate?

Yes, under the condition that there is not a meditator and nothing meditated on! In any case, there is awareness, without knowing it.

This is in relation to the question I asked yesterday. I could not express it clearly. You mentioned that truth and beauty give power and strength. Now, that is true, but talking in general in relation to society and myself, my experience shows that in society people hide truth and facts due to some selfish gain or something. People do not come up with truth and facts in the situation. And even myself, when I have to confront higher authorities like bosses or in some other situation where there is a certain amount of fear, or fear from the other party, I do not come out with the truth or facts as to what the real situation is. And that is what the other party does when I do business with them. What my question comes down to is: There is a certain amount of boldness and frankness needed to not hide the facts. That is one thing, and the second thing is: To get the same from the other party. In other words, fighting against evil, to need some kind of power and strength to fight against evil. And I do not find anybody talking with boldness and frankness. Even I cannot do it. So I am wondering how can we develop the strength and power to speak the truth.

The power comes out of truth itself which is beauty; there is power. Truth expresses itself in society in many forms.

Fighting could be non-violent or could be violent.

There is nothing wrong in fighting. There are many ways to fight. In a fighting situation, you cannot project a system of fighting. You cannot fight according to certain norms. Your tool must be ready, your arm must be relaxed, you must be completely aware, your feet must be strong, that belongs to the mechanism—but how to fight, you can only see what happens in the moment itself; you cannot project a way of fighting.

Still, even in the non-violence of Mahatma Gandhi who fought against the British, he would talk openly about the British kingdom being evil. He had some kind of guts or boldness or strength to talk that way. There was no one in India who could talk like that and that is why he was a leader. He could talk of facts and could put his life in front of them, that is what it amounts to. What do you suggest to develop that kind of strength and boldness?

When the ego is absent, all the intelligence and power of the universe are at your disposal. It depends completely on what kind of capital you have. You fight according to your capital. One cannot give a codified formula of when to act, how to act, when to fight or not to fight. It belongs to the situation itself. You act according to the situation. The power to act comes out of truth, out of your true nature. A systematic refusal to fight is also fighting.

Where does the capital come from?

The capital belongs to you. It is a gift given to you. And you fight and you live according to this capital. In the end you are in the society but you are not of the society. Society begins with you. But really, power and right acting come out of truth. I remind you of the *Bhagavad Gita*.

Your teaching helps our understanding mentally. What I do not understand is whether there is something we have to learn with our minds? Sometimes I sit and inquire and try to reflect about my life and its purpose and what to do, things like that. I have always given credence to these reflections, as though from them I would have an understanding and build something, perhaps become more mature, perhaps become more available to openness. Is there any value in doing this?

You must be really realistic. Start from the position in which you find yourself at this moment. Go back home and look at your activities, your surroundings. You will see that they are more or less fixed patterns. Look at them again from the welcoming point of view, and you will see which activities belong to you as a husband, which as a father, as a business-man, as a man who must earn a living. Face the problems of life—this belongs to you.

See all these activities from the welcoming point of view and you will be really astonished. Many things will come to the surface of your consciousness that you never saw before, because you were living only in patterns, in fixed forms. These elements that surface bring a complete rectification in your life. From these elements comes understanding and it is from the understanding that change comes. It is an organic change. See all your activities from the welcoming point of view. In this welcoming point of view there is no bargaining of like and dislike. Be very alert to the parasite, the "me," who will inevitably put this new position—which comes from life itself—into question. Do not go in this doubt. When there is a decision that comes from life, this decision is instantaneous. It does not go through the analytical mind; it comes from the situation itself. The solution comes directly from the situation. It is the only way—spiritual, practical, realistic—to behave. Otherwise, you remain enclosed in a kind of conceptual universe which you try to escape because there is no comfort in it, no freedom, no peace. You try new philosophies, new books, a new belief, a new wife, a new job, and so on, but all this keeps you still in the same universe.

When you really see the pattern which keeps you in this conceptual universe, there is a moment when you find yourself outside of the cage. In the welcoming position, if you can call it a position, you are out of the cage. You may see residues of the cage around you, but you are no longer in the cage. Of course, when you see things very clearly in this completeness, there are some practical changes that ask to be made, but I think you will manage it. You must have the conviction that you have the capital, the energy, to effect all that is required. When you do not have the energy or talent to effect something, then inquire where you can find it.

When you try to change your life from the point of view of the split mind, of like and dislike, the conflict remains. You may change the position of your writing table to face east or your bed towards the north. You may change your ways of doing many things, but the conflict in you still remains. You are involved in the furniture of life. You are wasting your energy with trivia.

What you call the anecdotal instead of the essential.

Exactly.

Do you experience a passion for all humanity to be awakened?

There must be the deep desire to be free. This is absolutely necessary.

Do you experience a longing that all should be awake?

I think the deep feeling, the deep desire to be free comes from freedom itself. Otherwise, from where can it come? You must live with it.

Yes, but I am asking you whether you feel you really want all of humanity to understand this?

Of course, of course, of course. Absolutely.

I'm experiencing these patterns you are talking about. They seem very clear to me and they all seem to go nowhere. There is no satisfaction. Dissatisfaction is part of the pattern, satisfaction is part of the pattern, there is no fulfillment. What do you suggest doing?

I would say don't forget what you have sometimes felt at our meeting; don't forget it. The words you can forget, but there is something more than the words.

You put everything in such a beautiful nutshell, I want to write it down, hold it. Because then I think I have it.

When you write it down, you lose it.

But can I be sure it will be there?

Absolutely sure.

It is like taping programs off the TV that you want to watch and then you never watch them because you know you have them.

[Another questioner] You have never used the word "God" since I have been here. I have a problem with that word. Can you tell me what that word means to you, or how you understand it?

The word means nothing to me, because it is a concept. This concept produces certain representations, certain feelings, but it remains a concept, a representation. In a certain way, when

40

you are stuck to the word, you insult God. So, I would say the absolute understanding is that you must see it is only in the absolute absence of yourself that there is God. As long as there is a self, God has no place in you and remains a concept. Have you heard the Buddhist saying, "If you meet the Buddha on the road, kill him"? It means: Kill the concept; go away from the concept.

Could you elaborate on the distinction between the blank state and true silence or the natural non-state?

Very often the progressive way emphasizes purifications and eliminations of the body and the mind, striving for beautiful feelings, beautiful emotions, sensations, beautiful thoughts, and so on. But this keeps you in the relation of observer and observed, the subject-object relationship. Then, when you come to the so-called last level of purification, you are so accustomed to the subject-object relationship that you cannot free yourself from it, so that when you come to the elimination of the last object you find it is a blank state. Being stuck in the blank state is a great tragedy, and it needs a really tremendous "appearing" in your life to come out of this subject-object relationship. Otherwise, it remains an enigma.

In this direct teaching, we face the ultimate immediately. We never see the body, senses and mind except through the ultimate. The purification comes from above to below. The ultimate is always in the background. Then, to awaken yourself in this silent oneness is a spontaneous event.

But if you are stuck in the blank state, welcome it. When you really welcome it, you will become aware of the mechanisms and see that all your energy is eccentric. The premise behind the progressive method, no matter how subtle, is that there is something to attain, something to find, something to achieve. In the direct method we absolutely know that there is nothing to attain, that what we are looking for, we are already. So, when you are completely relaxed in this blank state, welcoming it, you will feel you are open to the welcoming, open to the openness. Welcoming welcomes its own welcoming. Welcoming refers to itself spontaneously, without any agent, without any middleman. There is no other way to proceed. In living open to the openness, open to *being* the openness, you are at the threshhold of being taken in your real nature.

July 15

Yesterday you talked about the heart being perhaps the final frontier. I wonder if you might elaborate on the heart.

The heart is still a localization, but there, you are at the threshold of Reality. It is the last going out, I would say. But the localization of your heart is still a localization.

When you say "heart" do you mean the feeling of love that sits in that place?

I am not speaking of the physiological heart, of course. It is a place where there is a sacred feeling, but one should hear this and immediately forget it.

I think you once said that the silent mind is the final barrier that the yogi has which keeps him still in duality. You said the silent mind is still an object.

Oh, yes.

How can that be understood? Is it that there are different qualities of emptiness, different qualities of stillness?

What you call a mind does not exist. The mind is a number

43

of functions, a number of qualities. When these functions come to a stop, because there are moments in life when we do not use the mind, then there is an absence of functions. But this absence of function is not the silence we mean here. The mind may be silent from time to time, but the nature of our mind is function. To concentrate on the stillness of the mind may give you a certain relaxation, but this in itself is a state, a blank state. We are not speaking of this emptiness. We are speaking of an emptiness without duration, without time.

It is very difficult for us to represent space without a center and without a periphery. When you look out of the window here, you first see trees, bushes, meadows, stars, the moon. You look at objects in relation to other objects, but you never notice the space in which the objects exist. Your looking is a kind of comparison. You know yourself only in objects because you relate with your personality which is an object too. So what is important for you is to experience the absence of all objects, including your center, your personality. Your presence is in the absence of all objects. In other words, you are really present only in your absence. Do you see what I mean?

It is important that the mind sees this kind of geometrical representation. Your absence can never be represented. You cannot think it or feel it. That is why, in reality, metaphysically speaking, we can never name it, we can only express it negatively. We can only express our reality negatively, never positively. What we are fundamentally is our absence. And when you ask how can you experience your absence, you cannot experience it, because it is in the absence of the experiencer. Your absence is your wholeness. When obliged to give a description, one could say, "It is a feeling without feeling it."

It seems as though this feeling without feeling can be felt whether the object is there or not.

When you look, you look from the point of view of an object in subject-object relationship, but if this last object, the subject-I, disappears, then you are in your wholeness, absence, space.

When there are no thoughts present in the mind, no thoughts about an object, subject, or anything, does that mean you are fully present to the situation?

Time and space are created by thoughts. When there is an absence of thoughts, generally we feel or think the absence, we make it an object and still project a possible presence. So we must come to the absence of the absence, the double absence.

During yoga today you talked about releasing "the parasites," and I'd never heard you use this term before. You said to let go of the parasites on the exhalation.

When you do the movement there may be some compensations or reactions to the movement. These compensations or reactions are, for me, parasites. When you find the position and relax it a little, you give up these parasites; you empty the space, you empty the movement. Then do it again until the movement is completely empty, free of parasites. Do you see what I mean? Because a real movement must be fulfilled with feeling. When the movement is fulfilled with feeling it is no longer mechanical. It is the same when you see art on stage, dance which expresses itself in movement. When the movement is empty, it has no meaning. From the outside the movement is there, there is the right architecture in space, but it is empty. It gives you no joy. Look at the Bolshoi or most ballet companies. Very often of the twenty or so dancers there are only one or two in whom the movement is really fulfilled. So when we say "the parasites must go away" we mean the reactions must be eliminated, and then the movement is fulfilled.

A parasite is something that lives off something else, depends on a host for its energy, and so...

Yes, the host is memory. It is a memory.

And so they take energy.

Try, when doing the movements to empty the movements. As long as there is intentional power, energy which remains even as memory, as residue, you are involved in it and can never take note of it, can never take it as a fact. Unless the movement is empty, it cannot be realized. When I said "parasite" it was more or less a poetic expression. Sometimes one needs some words to shock people. No?

So, is there a quality, other than just being aware of the movement, that you are trying to achieve by eliminating the parasites?

Yes. As long as there are parasites, you do not give up and empty the movement to give place to the feeling. There needs to be a giving-up. The moment you have the sensation that your arm is filled with feeling, perceived full of sensation, then you will see the muscles work completely differently. When I lift my arms vertically, there is the same feeling here, here, here, here. This is very easy, you can do it too. Then there come some complicated movements which are more difficult. You must be comfortable in all your movements.

What is important is not to emphasize the body, but to

realize that the body lives in awareness. There is a difference when you do a movement or a posture and you are completely involved in it, completely stuck to it, and when it unfolds in awareness.

If the mind is in a quiet state, from experience we know that the mind and the personality will come back. The state of absence of the person is not permanent and the person returns. If in the thought-free state any effort is made to maintain it, this effort is an action of the person.

Absolutely.

But if no effort is made the person will return.

To maintain an absence of activity, to maintain a still mind calls for effort. When you enforce a still mind you go to sleep.

So here is the dilemma.

The moment you sustain your attention you go deeper.

That's an effort.

It is not an effort. You live freely; you are effortless, because you take it for granted that your natural, absolute atomic state is completely peaceful, completely without effort. This be-ingness is your natural atomic state.

So there should be a kind of willingness to yield to a still deeper state.

You can never go to the original state because you are it. You can only give up what you are not. The moment you know what you are not, there is a natural giving-up. What remains, if we can still say that something remains, can never be named, never explained. Any word you could find would be a thought, a type of representation.

When the thought has no more capacity to represent, it gives up. You do not give it up; it gives itself up. Take time with our conversation. All the activities of your mind and body appear in your space, appear in your consciousness, in your timelessness.

So you are saying, "You are the consciousness and everything appears in it"?

Yes. All objects, all that is perceived, all that exists, appears in consciousness. That is why we say that all that is perceived, all that exists, has no existence in itself because it depends on consciousness. Consciousness and its object are one. You can never have two objects at the same time. There is only one object. So an object has no reality in itself, no existence in itself. It refers to consciousness. The object appears in space and time, but consciousness does not move. Objectless consciousness is unthinkable for many people.

How does it help us to know that there can only be one object in consciousness at a time? What does that show?

The moment you know that an object exists only because you are conscious, that an object cannot be known without consciousness and that consciousness and its object are one, then you are ejected into the unthinkable. You are brought back to the "I" that cannot be thought and all you can do is find yourself in the unthinkable.

It is very easy for my mind to make an object out of anything.

48

But even when you speak of the ego, of the "I," the "I" is only related to situations as an object: I am hungry, I am cold, I am depressed, I am stiff, I am old. The "I" exists only in relation to situations and objects. When you take away the situation, you can never think "I." This pronoun "I," standing alone without qualification, can never be thought. It refers directly to the unthinkable. You cannot represent the "I."

Yesterday, you gave an exercise where we unfocussed our eyes and located the attention in the back of the neck. In investigating this I found objects not to be static, but dynamic. Then someone came by and immediately my attention changed to perceiving objects in the usual hard static way. When the exercise was repeated there was an experience of palpable resistance. It seemed like I needed—this is probably the wrong word—a certain kind of "will." Not an ego-will, but a will of another quality or kind. Would you comment?

But look, when in one moment you realized that you know only what is knowable, that all you really know is the knowable, when you take that as a fact, there is a moment that you feel yourself completely out of the cage of the known. When you take it as a fact that you only know yourself in the knowable, you are automatically brought back to not-knowing where there is no experiencer and nothing is experienced. You feel yourself in the non-state where there is not a knower and nothing is known. Do you follow me?

In what we were pursuing a moment ago, it seems like you are touching on it again. We can be in consciousness, merely being, but then it seems that that attention is thrown out by the mind which pulls us away from that inner being; then somehow we are confused again. So we search and relocate that feeling of being, but it is constantly being thrown out. Is it a question of continuing to come back to that inner being? Or will it always be thrown out?

Live knowingly in your absence. It is really in your absence that there is presence, and the rest is functioning. In this absence of yourself you live in a non-qualified state. You function as a father, as a lover, a teacher, a driver and so on, simply functioning. But you do not take yourself for a driver, a doctor, a teacher, a father. You simply function. So in all the circumstances of functioning refer to your absence. There is no more choice. You are no longer in the psychological structure of shame, like and dislike, of choice.

But what is important is that the moment you take note, take it as a fact that you only know yourself in the knowable, you must sustain the moment of this insight; live this moment completely. This moment is timeless and refers to itself. The stopping in this moment refers to the not-knowing, the welcoming non-state. It is the original perception where there is not a perceiver and nothing is perceived. It is an apperception of reality.

What is the relation between the witness state and the non-state?

As long as there is a subject and an object—I speak of the relative subject—there is a witness. When you see that the subject is nothing other than an object too, then in the merging of object-subject the witness also disappears and there is only consciousness.

After an action you can only say that many things appeared and I was witness to them. It is important that you say, after an action: I was not the actor, I was not the doer, I was witness to it. This helps you to go out of the recording to be an actor, to be a doer. At the time of acting there is only action, only function. You live completely out of psychological time.

The moment that you take it as a fact that you live only in

the knowable, then I would say the fact refers to you. It reveals the ultimate, it reveals your presence. And how you live this presence, I cannot explain. One can only say you have the impression that in this presence all is included. Nothing is outside. There is nothing else.

I think the nearest is when you speak of love. I mean when you speak of love in an earnest way, not what we call romantic love. In love there is no border, no center, no object, no lover; there is not a beloved, there is just love. You are nowhere, but you can say "I am everywhere."

What is the basis of action? How do we know when to go, or to move?

It is the divine who acts through you. You are more or less a child. You just act. When you look out of the window and you realize that all the objects that you see live in this surrounding space, artistically speaking, identify yourself completely with the space, and from the space, look again at the object. You will see it has a completely new aspect. You will see yourself extended in this space. You *are* the space.

Would it be the same as in painting? The space forms the object.

When you go into a cathedral and see all the stained glass windows, these windows express the lives of the saints, people with wisdom, and so on, but all the history that is expressed in the stained glass is visible only through the light that comes from outside; otherwise what kind of stained glass is it? The same is true of our life which only has significance with this light, our light.

As I am able to see that beliefs, feelings or emotions are just in that moment and refer back to the space, then those begin to have no more hold on me, so that there is the continual ongoing sense that everything is coming and going inside me.

Yes, yes. Everything lives in you and every thought comes out of the silence and refers to silence. There is no more psychological living. In this emptiness there is emotion, I would say there is sacredness, but there is no more emotivity. Emotion is giving, it is expression, it is beauty, but emotivity is a defense.

When the fact refers to your wholeness, to your completeness, it reveals you. And how you live the revealing, how you live the moment when reality reveals itself, we cannot formulate. It is stronger and more real than touching the ground, but we cannot explain it. It is our nearest.

I can express it: Memory lives in me; I do not live in the memory.

Absolutely. This is not an abstract concept.

Is this what you are doing in the asana at the end when you held the pose and you said, "Now stop the movement; take it as a fact"? What I feel is the dissolving of any ideal images I might be holding of where I think I'm moving. It is like a dissolving of memory. It is almost as if the body itself begins to dissolve and then there is just being in that position, or rather the position is in being. But the essence is probably that one allows the memory and the ideal images just to dissolve. Is that so?

Yes. It comes from you and goes to you. It comes from you; it refers to you. There is only one. Oneness expresses itself through oneness. God enjoys itself through itself, by itself.

Once one is established in one's presence, the original nature, I assume it is a dynamic and not a static experience. Is there

some—words are very difficult here—is there some enrichment
of that experience of presence? Does love grow more or is it
complete with that first realization? ·

In real love in this timeless awareness there is no evolution, there
is no progression. If we can speak of a starting point, it is to
acquaint oneself with this thought-free perception. In this
thought-free perception the perception unfolds completely and
our attention unfolds completely, and then intelligence unfolds
and total sensitivity—call it awareness. First you are aware of
something, and then you become aware that you are aware. You
will also see that being aware of awareness is when there is an
absence of any object, and you can speak of objectless awareness.
Then you come back to the senses again, and there is awareness
with an object. But generally, what we call an object is not an
object. It is an expression of your awareness. When the object
refers to its homeground, it loses its profanity and is sacred. So,
of course, all objects are sacred.

So the love and the insight are complete in one moment, but the
manifestation of love or the manifestation of the insight in the
teaching form or in the world, do these change over time?

Love that comes directly from Love has the power to change
things dramatically.

So the form of one's life will change radically.

Oh, yes, the way you express it, the sensitivity. It becomes
precise. It has even a kind of logic. Of course, it depends on
one's temperament. You may express it in a different way than
I or she, but its homeground is the same. The expression can
take many forms and these are never exhausted. The expressions of love are constantly new, never come to an end.

In that sense then you no longer see vulgarity.

No, no. Vulgarity is seen only by the mind.

But the mind can see it.

Who can see it?

But vulgarity does not affect you if you are not an object; you do not identify as an object, so it has no effect, in a sense.

[Another questioner] A lot of the questions so far I find very intellectual, very cerebral. Is it important to ask these questions of myself, or is just living with myself and watching what I do enough?

When questions come up, take your questions seriously. Do not try immediately to answer through the already known—through your memory. Live with your question simply, but do not try to find the question. In observing your life and observing your surroundings questions may come up, questions like "What is life?" There comes a moment in life when you make a kind of balance sheet. Then you go through all the numbers on the balance sheet. And then when you come to the end you ask yourself, "Is this really life? Is this all there is? I have done so many occupations; I have seen so many girl friends; I have been to so many places. Is this really life?" Do not try to give an answer. Do not try even to find an answer in you. Only see things as a fact. But do not emphasize the fact. When you emphasize the fact you remain with the fact. You can only see a fact when you stay outside of it. When you are on the platform and you see the train rushing by at eighty miles an hour, you are out of the movement and can see it clearly. When you are in the train you cannot see the speed.

The moment you see a fact it refers immediately to your timeless presence. It reveals your timeless presence and vanishes in your timeless presence. Live with it. It is very strong when the fact refers to your presence.

July 16

Truth never changes, but the expressions of truth are constantly in change, continually new. It is only the "person" who, looking for security, turns life into repetition. In reality, there is analogy between moments, but there is no repetition. When you face life you must never look at it through memory. Be free from memory. You bring certain aptitudes into play, aptitudes from heredity, father, mother, and also certain learned tools, ways of behavior acquired through your education and experience. All this belongs to your personality. In facing life without memory and accepting totally the facts, you find yourself open to life. In this openness there is intelligence, in this openness there is sensitivity. So the real personality comes from the moment itself, from the situation itself. There is nothing personal about intelligence and sensitivity. The real personality arises with the situation and dissolves with the situation, leaving no residue. You are free from memory. There is no compromise. You act according to the situation. So there is nothing personal in the real personality. When you act according to the situation, it is action without will, free from the ego. In other words, real action is looking away from the personal action. You must look away from the target. To obtain the goal you must look away from the goal.

The usual way I encounter a situation is with a sense of insecurity.

I understand from what you say that this is because I've forgotten who I am, my real self, therefore I'm insecure. Now, I don't understand what you mean by saying that in action we look away. Do we look away from the past, or do we look away from the situation we see in front of us, and see it empty?

Look away from memory. Alan Watts wrote in a beautiful book many years ago, *The Wisdom of Insecurity*, "Real security is insecurity." That means that there is a perfect insecurity for the I, and in accepting this, there is security. There is only security in the egoless state. Life meets you constantly in a new way. We put it in a framework of previous moments, but when we know we project the already known, then we must give it up. We can see immediately that we have taken a direction that does not belong to the situation. Real thinking is looking away from thinking. Real acting is looking away from acting.

Do we call certain situations to ourselves in order to learn the next step in expansion?

When you see the situation from a certain point of view, like or dislike, then you act according to your like. Then you can never really face a situation. You must face a situation with your choiceless observation.

I think I understand your words, but what's happening is that I find this pattern of reactions already in momentum in a situation and it's as though it's happening to somebody else who's going through old patterns, old memories, manipulation, silly things for his own purpose, and I'm watching it from outside. I want to shake him from this foolishness, because it's not even a person, just a series of gestures. It's like looking at a stranger.

When you act according to your like and dislike, you live in the past and you are isolated from the present situation. Free from psychological memory, you are one with the situation, and the action in this situation leaves no residue. In the transpersonality which comes from heredity, from what you have learned in school, your experience, your desire to be a perfect artisan, there remains something functional. But the elements required to really face the situation with intelligence and sensitivity come from the situation itself.

Is it the element of insecurity that makes me keep calling on memory, keeps one relying on memory?

Yes, because we cannot find our familiar selves in waiting. The actor who goes on stage with memory is never a good actor. The real actor has the feeling of his role, of the global feeling of his play. But he doesn't rely on memory. There may be a kind of excitement, but this excitement is a sacred excitement; it comes from the play that is performed itself. The excitement from the I-image is really destructive. The excitement that comes from the play is completely different. So, in life it is the same.

We keep operating in the circle of personality and memory and our true personality can only be realized by being open to the situation. I want to say that there must be a way to find a vehicle or a medium to be open, but that's just going back into the personality.

One can never face life appropriately with the already known. We repeat life but life never repeats. Why superimpose repetition on what is constantly original?

In my own personal life, when a new situation arises, the first feeling I have is that of fear. I can imagine myself in the state of being at that moment without fear, but I am not sure how to achieve it. I seem to have two choices—to embrace my fear, see the person who is afraid and lovingly embrace him and hold it. The other way seems to be to put it aside and put myself in another frame of mind that states, "This is a new occurrence. It is happening right now. I am in the moment. I will act." Are both of these authentic or am I trying to push away the memory of the person, the ego in the second state?

Something happens before you notice the fear. There is a moment when you see the situation in relation to your personality, your ego, and then you are afraid. So the fear belongs to what, really? It does not come from the situation. There may also be anticipation that the person will not immediately find, through memory, the power to face the situation. The ego anticipates a failure; "I may not be a hero in this situation." Then the fear comes in even before the situation arises. It has already taken place in you. You must face the ground of the fear.

How?

When you are not in a crisis of fear, inquire. Inquire "Who is afraid? Who has fear? Who anticipates?" You will never find this "who" and you will see it is an illusion. Once you are in a state of fear, then look at it pragmatically, objectively like a scientist. To do this you need to accept the fear. When you accept the fear you are out of the process of fear and as you are out of the process, the fear cannot remain as a fixed energy. It dissolves in your acceptance. Then look at the situation again. This second looking is important. Take the opportunity to look at the situation from the completely impersonal point of view, from your globality, from your totality.

When I think of accepting my fear, I get even more frightened.

You are still emphasizing the object and growing it, feeding it. In real acceptance, you do not emphasize accepting the fear, the object, but you remember the accepting itself. The object is emphasized only long enough to bring you back to the subject, accepting. The object is a pointer to its accepting. When you accept the fear, you are free from the fear.

You mean you accept being fearful?

In accepting the fear, you are not in the fear, the fear is in you, and the fear cannot live because you find yourself in a state where there is no place for a person to maintain and feed the fear. With this glimpse of freedom from fear, look at the situation again. When you explore fear several times in this way, you will see that you become aware of the situation even before the person reacts. The person may still come in, but much later. This delay is important.

Is there an element of surrender in acceptance?

Absolutely, complete surrender, but not in a fatalistic sense. You must experience it.

When there's acceptance of fear or anger, does this dissolve the fear or anger before it is manifest? Do I try to stop it or does it stop of its own accord before it comes out? Or is it alright if it does come out and I still accept it and let it go?

You feel the moment the anger has taken place in you. From then on when you try to justify the anger or to rationalize or argue it, everything you do only contributes to the anger. When you really see that no technique, no system, no new element can take away the anger, and, in fact, only constantly feeds it, then you accept the anger. In accepting it really, you will see there comes a kind of transfer. Whereas before, you constantly emphasized the anger, in this transfer the power which you used to emphasize the anger goes back to the acceptance and you will emphasize the acceptance itself. And then there is something wondrous. You will see that acceptance is not bound to what is accepted. Acceptance exists in itself, is completely free from what it accepts, and refers to itself. Feel this accepting state. How do you feel? You are completely free. Being aware of this free feeling is most important because you will know with conviction that you are no longer completely stuck to, bound to the anger. And see what happens in this moment. When you accept the anger you are not in the anger, the anger is in you, and as you are in this acceptance, this totality, this emptying, there is no longer a possibility of feeling the anger. It dissolves, because it is nothing other than energy. When you really deal with anger, you will see it is a pointer to your real nature, to your real center. In any case, what you are really looking for in life is to find the center from which you function, love, act, think, do. You are looking for a center.

The word accepting is conditioned. It has a little bad taste, let us say. Accepting is grim, it is a heavy word, too much weight. Perhaps it is better not to use it. So a better word is welcoming.

In welcoming, automatically the word refers to itself, its openness, receptivity. In welcoming you are already receptive.

I'm trying to work with spots in my body that are tense, and trying to let them dissolve. There's a little release in the throat, then I go to the back. But by the time I get back to the throat it's constricted again.

Your body is your vehicle, it's your tool. You need it for acting. You must explore it. In exploring it you will see it is conditioned through previous action, previous reactions. What we call our body is mainly only a field of reactions from previous situations, childhood and so on. So when you face your vehicle, your body, you will see there are residues of resistance in it. Explore where the resistances are, in the same way as we have been talking about here—emphasizing the accepting itself—and there comes a moment when you are free from this resistance and will use your body in a completely different way. We were often angry yesterday but today we are not angry, yet there are still residues of the anger very deep in the body. These residues form the muscle and nervous tensions in the body. Face these tensions directly without analyzing their origin.

Become acquainted with your body, first in non-action, lying down and sitting. See how the zones of which you are conscious appear to you. You will find many zones you are not aware of. So there comes a kind of palate of sensation, of feeling. Certain parts are completely light, transparent, others heavy and dense. Then in a certain way, you need to choose to emphasize the zones that are completely empty. Familiarize yourself with the empty feeling, then invade with the empty sensation, the other tense zones. In this way, you come to a kind of homogeneous feeling of your body. You first come to this feeling in a situation where there is no action, when lying down for example, then you can keep this homogeneous feeling, I would say this healthy feeling, in action. Whether it's the art of singing or walking, or playing music, or jogging or fighting, you have a relaxed unconditioned body ready for action. Look at the people jogging on your street. They don't know how to run. A relaxed body must be employed in action. You know that book *Zen in the Art of Archery*? It is very interesting. You must not be affected by all the residues from past actions. In a certain way he spoke of deconditioning the body.

Coming back to the question that every situation is new, free from psychological memory, like a good actor…but in his psychological memory he has years of experience. If he makes that memory flexible rather than rigid and depending upon the new situation he acts, is that what you mean by free from psychological memory?

You face the situation in a choiceless state. This means you accept, you welcome the situation. In this moment, the situation refers to your acceptance, to your welcoming. The situation articulates itself completely. And this situation brings its own solution, its own acting. There is no reacting. The acting comes out of the situation itself. Intelligence and sensitivity come out of the situation. It is the situation which, in a certain way, builds in you the personality which belongs to the moment itself. The action comes out of the situation itself. To act really you must look away from acting, be free from the notion of acting.

But the actor should be prepared through training and experience to handle that situation.

He must be an artisan. He has learned how to speak, how to pronounce, he has undertaken voice culture, pronunciation, body behavior, all this belongs to the profession.

Profession is psychological memory, right?

No, no, no, functional memory. It doesn't need to be remembered at all times. It comes up in the moment itself, when you need it. When you're thirsty, you drink.

I'm still not clear on looking away from acting.

Looking away from acting means looking away from willful acting, being free from the ego. There is no intention, no strategy. The moment you look at the situation from the personal point of view, it becomes a psychological problem, a conflict.

There are a lot of choices, right? Is choice a function?

See how you yourself function. When you face a situation, see immediately that choice comes up. When it gives you security or pleasure, you identify yourself with it. When it does not give security or pleasure, you push it into the unconscious, or you push it away. So in both situations, in identification with the situation as well as in pushing it away, in both the situations, you are isolated, not one with the situation. That you must see.

Can you differentiate between ego and personality?

Ego and personality are the same. Psychological memory belongs to the personality. It is only to create a number of securities for the person. When the reflex for psychological security leaves you, the psychological aspect of the personality also goes away and only the functional aspect remains. When you live in psychological time, you live only in anticipation, past future, past future; you are never present.

What about individuality? What makes us different from one another?

The moment you face the situation from your personal point of view you can be sure there is conflict, there is choice. The moment the notion of being a personal entity goes away, you live completely in your openness, in your emptiness. Everything that appears in your life refers to this emptiness. Then there is really functional behavior.

So functional behavior brings in all one's innate talents, intelligence and sensitivity. It explores the range of human possibilities. But psychological conditioned behavior, being limited, is sheeplike and restricted in expression. Are we not more different, unique, when we function freely than when we function in bondage?

Absolutely.

I have some further questions about choice. When in conflict, I clearly see it's my mind in conflict. Once that conflict is seen, is it sometimes necessary that the mind has to make a choice, or with greater awareness, is it possible to go beyond the conflict so that the decision or action that's required, especially about something in the future, can come from the totality?

Timeless awareness is beyond choice.

So in some respects choice doesn't matter, which direction...

There is no personal choice. There may be action, but it does not go through the mind.

The solution to the situation is beyond choice.

Absolutely.

If the spontaneous understanding comes up to indicate a certain direction, but the time to act isn't yet, should you always stay with the original intuition?

The action is instantaneous. The understanding is instantaneous, but the realization of the intuition is in time and space.

But by then do you have to remember the original?

No, you must live with the intuition.

So you keep it alive.

Yes. It is the intuition that helps you to realize the action in space and time. It is very important.

But how do you keep the intuition alive without it being memory?

The intuition has nothing to do with memory. Intuition is a global feeling. When you're an artist, and you have a real picture to express, you live a long time with the picture to realize it in space and time. Very often when you lose the intuition, the mind comes in, calculation comes in, and you are not in the direction. I think you can see it in history. In many situations you can see where there was intuition, one went to a certain point, and then calculation and intention, the mind, the person came in. Then comes the conflict, the struggle.

You see that in religious traditions.

Oh absolutely, you can see it in the Catholic system. Very precisely, you saw it in the meeting in Constantinople when the Roman Church separated from the Greek Orthodox Church. It was a big conflict for the church. It was a choice through reasoning, not intuition. You also have a similar separation in Buddhism between the Hinayana and Mahayana.

What is the relationship of intimidation and fear? When you meet a physically powerful person there is a certain kind of intimidation. But even more intimidating is when you meet a very powerful personality. Then I lose a sense of what is happening.

In the first situation it is biological survival. In the second it is psychological survival.

But the response to the psychological survival is total breakdown. It seems to be a very poor response.

Biological survival is completely normal, in a certain way. But psychological survival is completely an illusion.

How would you view that situation? Where's the reality, and what's the illusion?

The illusion is that you take yourself for somebody. Free yourself of the notion of being somebody. You must not only have the idea that you are nothing, but you must be alive in this nothingness. In this nothingness, psychological survival has no meaning.

There's nobody to protect?

You're a very competitive man, that you know. You take a certain pleasure in competition, that you know. You like to fight. You like to be the hero, to come out as the winner of the battlefield.

Should I not have that feeling? Is it wrong to play to win as opposed to playing for playing's sake?

Playing is for the love of playing, simply playing. The pleasure is in doing it.

So I guess from your answer that there is an alternative way of being—other than competitive. What is it?

Real being is in your emptiness and when life asks you to face a moment, then you really face the moment. You are open for something which is beyond your psychological memory. Psychological memory is very little, very limited in fulfilling what the situation needs from you. It is very inadequate. The moment you are completely open to the situation, you will see how rich you are. But this richness does not belong to you, it belongs to the cosmos, to the world.

You've sometimes talked about the cosmic personality. Referring back to the previous question, in terms of Jung, in terms of deep psychological structure, each of us is living out a myth, some archetype, and Jung's idea of the highest archetype would be the Solar Hero, Jesus becoming Christ. Now as one comes through their psychological manifestation, they begin to see that they always take a certain stance in a situation, either of a hero, or conciliator, or whatever these myths or archetypes are. And so many of us, being afflicted, do not really live that through. Is there anything to this Jungian perception?

I think in this way, every being occupies a place in this cosmic web. Everyone is a link in the chain. The whole web is everywhere. There is nothing outside. Everything that has been, that should come, is already in our cells, I would say. All that has been and what should come is already in the now. There is no past, there is no future, there is only now. Our brain functions in past-future, memory. But in reality, that only belongs to our brain function. We live in the now. It is perfect simultaneity. The film is in one moment. The film goes on in space and time but the film is actually here. So I would say we have in us all totality: Egyptians, Chinese, all our history, all our past is in us. In a way we have a certain role to play. Everything is in the film, but we are the light that illumines the screen. We are not on the screen. So what is on the screen is more or less a pretext that points back to our light. Whether you believe it or not is also on the film!

Is the film already made? Does it already exist?

In a certain way, I would say the film is already made, but from the ultimate view, the film is made from moment to moment. It is difficult for our minds to grasp, that at the same time the film is already made and that the film gets made from moment to moment.

We follow the direct path, and for the ten years I've known you, I feel that I've been ready. I've been listening to talks, doing yoga, learning to breathe, and I know that my personality is not going to get...

Oh, I like this question. Be a little more aggressive.

I know my mind is not going to get it, my body is not going to get it, I am what I want to be and there is nothing to strive for. Of course I could read more about the lives of the saints, I could do more yoga, but I heard you once say to somebody, "I offer you enlightenment, see that you refuse it." If I am already what I'm striving for, I want enlightenment now.

You can have it, but you must immediately see the cost of it, the price.

I don't see any price. I could see it a few years ago. I don't feel like there's any fear of the price anymore. I've seen the uselessness of my desires, of being the personality. Therefore I accept the personality for functional purposes, but there's really that desire for surrender to beauty and love. This is clear. However, I also see that I am not enlightened. I want to be. My mind says, "Don't be arrogant." My heart says, "Why wait?" Of course, my body still has certain things; my mind is not peaceful. How can I still go on and find my axis?

When you see it in the moment itself, there is understanding. But I think later, there may come in again a kind of bargaining. That you should see also. But when you have seen it once, you may be sure you will be solicited in other moments.

And from that solicitation to solicitation....

You may come to the establishment.

July 17—morning

Stillness has nothing to do with consciousness or unconsciousness. Stillness is the room here without objects, without even the walls. The objects appear in stillness. When you see that an object refers to the totality that you are fundamentally, then the object has a completely different significance. You know the Zen saying certainly better than I do, the one where first, the ordinary person is completely involved in the mountain, sees it as a mountain; then there is a moment when there is a switchover and the seeing refers to itself, then there is no mountain, only awareness. Then he looks again at the mountain. There is still a mountain, but it is not a mountain in the same way as before because it refers to consciousness.

This means that the mountain is no longer isolated. It belongs to the looker. It does not mean that the object dissolves; the object is still there. But it is seen in consciousness. It becomes sacred. The moment it does not refer to totality, to your real being, it is vulgar, it is ordinary. But the moment it refers to your ultimate being, it is sacred.

In that sense, then, in the awareness of just being in the awareness, objects are continually arising, but that awareness is never relinquished, forgotten.

You can never forget it. This has nothing to do with memory.

I understand. I do not mean it in the way of memory. I mean that you are not; the object does not distract you.

Yes. Consciousness is a continuum.

If that is so, then what is the difference between the one who is aware of that and the one who is awake?

This awareness knows itself by itself. It does not need an agent, a middleman, to be known. You know it only in oneness, where there is no subject-object relationship. But the object is not autonomous, it needs consciousness to be known. When you understand something objective, you will see that there is a reflex to be stuck to the object. But to understand something that is not within the conceptual framework, you cannot be stuck to the objective understanding and you are brought back to *being* the understanding. In this being understanding there is no representation. There is no thinking. Do you see what I mean? You must observe how you function. When you come to the conviction that you understand something that is not thinkable, then it must bring you back. When you understand what is truth, what is unthinkable, it brings you back to the non-state where there is no representation, where you are not in subject-object relationship. You will even note changes on the organic level. Your forehead has no more role to play. You are taken behind you.

When you ask most people, "Who are you?" they say, "Well, I am the mind, or I am the body." But once you start looking, pretty soon you come to the conclusion: I am not this or that. I have reached a place where your teaching about acceptance seems to be taking on a lot of meaning for me. I have realized that when I say I am the body or the mind, the problem is that I have never claimed my body and my mind. When I watch my own mind it always seems to be in reaction to something. Even when I watch my body, my mind seems to handle the body sensation in terms of reaction or in terms of delay. And when I bring acceptance to these sensations, to what I used to call my world, it starts to dissolve. But what seems to block total dissolving is the sense of being a sinner, of being in the wrong, where all things seem to come to this sinner which I call myself. I experience this from a feeling level, not from a mental level. Is there any advantage in trying to be open to the perception of this center from a feeling level? I cannot get a hold of it on an intellectual level. Is there any advantage to accepting that sinner?

When you look at a thing, generally you are not even aware of it because there is immediately resistance, reaction. And this resistance creates another resistance, another reaction. In other words, you find yourself in a chain of reactions. But, when you become aware—and by becoming aware I mean seeing it with an innocent mind, with an innocent awareness, an innocent attention—when you become aware that you react, that you resist, then these reactions and this resistance no longer have an accomplice. This means there is no longer a subject-object which controls, evaluates, compares.

Automatically, then, this resistance and reaction, this energy unfolds and vanishes in your globality. The letting-go of resistance brings you back to your presence which can never be thought or touched. You can never...you can only say that it is more than all existence. Existence is in space and time, but this presence is beyond time and space. Live this dimension in the moment itself. Be completely attuned to it. By that I mean do not try to objectify it, do not try to touch it. When you try to make it touchable, it is already away.

[pause]

You are completely open to a new dimension. We know awareness only when it refers to objects. We do not know

75

awareness when it refers to itself. When it refers to itself, it is a new dimension, if you can even speak of a new dimension. It is like when I ask you what you have in your hand and you immediately say, "I have nothing in my hand." But you do have something in your hand. You have your hand in your hand. You have sensitivity in your hand. Your hand has its own feeling, its own hand, I would say. Or if I ask whether you have something in your mouth, you say, "No, I have nothing." But there is the taste of your mouth. To clarify this analogy: When the object is not there, consciousness has its own taste, I would say the real taste.

Once you totally taste that taste, the taste that you are, is that permanent? I mean, once you are...

Oh, absolutely! The taste has tasted its own taste. It knows that the real taste never goes away. It knows the background to all other tastes.

I have another teacher whom I also love. I have read recently that this can be a big mistake. Atmananda Krishna Menon referred to this. I was wondering if you could comment on this situation.

Life is the best teacher. Every circumstance, in a certain way, is a teacher. I think every situation, every moment brings you to a question. You have to deal with situations, with objects, and every situation, every moment can bring you back to the "Who am I?" What is this "I" that you can never represent? What is the fundamental global feeling of "I"? You can never concretize it, but still there is a kind of original feeling. So, every moment of every situation can bring you back to this inquiry. And what happens then, is that you live in an unknown.

The problem is that when you find yourself in the "I don't

know" there is still the reflex to know. In your not-knowing you are still fixed to a possible knowable. The awareness that there is still a goal in your not-knowing may be the Teacher. Otherwise, all your life you will be stuck with this possible knowable which is actually a blank state. But when the question comes up to ask "Who am I?" and you come to the real "I don't know," then there is an up-giving, a giving-up of all that is knowable. And then you are living in waiting without waiting. It is an opening, and you will feel, without feeling it, that openness has its own taste.

You said that every moment can bring us back to the inquiry, "Who am I?" or the inquiry into our real nature. Should we consciously let all objects do this, refer all situations to this inquiry as a kind of sadhana, or is it a matter of accident that one day I will wake up and all situations will refer to the global "I"?

It is not an accident. You will find certain moments when you are available to it.

So in part what you are saying is that this dilemma I present is only a function of taking myself as a student?

Yes.

That if I approach life from the open and impersonal perspective, then life will be my teacher?

Do not take yourself for a professional disciple. [laughter]

Jean, the gift then seems, as you are saying it, to be the taste.

Yes, yes.

It is the consciousness knowing itself. That's it. It is the hand feeling itself. And then living in that taste.

Yes.

Can one move towards that sensation, that taste? Is this taste that we can go towards maybe the final sensation?

You cannot go to it. You can go *toward* to a certain extent, but then you are involuntarily consumed in a certain way. The explorer is consumed. You disappear. Only in the absolute disappearance of the person is there the taste.

So the taste stands without duality.

Without duality. I can tell an experience that occurred when I was about seventeen years old, where the ego was consumed. I was returning home after completing some work and I was completely satisfied. There was nothing more to add or change. It was finished work. I was at the station waiting for a train and it was announced that the train was going to run twenty-five minutes late. Now, it was a fact that the train would be twenty-five minutes late and that there was nothing to do to produce the train. That I had done my work was a fact, too. So it was a moment when I was completely without expectation, wishing, without exploring anything at all. I found myself in absolute nothingness. But I did not know myself in this nothingness.

Then a cock [rooster] crowed, even though it was two o'clock in the afternoon. And in this moment my attention was taken by the sound of the cock and I was aware that there was silence around the sound. The cry of the cock made me aware of the silence, not only the objective silence of the countryside but the absolute tranquillity within. This event echoed in me for many, many years. It left a kind of organic memory. It brought me to more than an experience. It is very important that you become aware, through the object, that you are in silence, in being.

This is an example, then, of the object pointing back to silence, its source.

Yes.

You were speaking before about waiting. My mind was saying: Why doesn't he say receiving? An image suddenly struck me of a bus stop, with someone who needed to get somewhere and kept looking and walking back and forth and all of that, trying to hurry the bus, and I was just watching him. And it seems it is very sly, because the waiting ultimately erases the observer in the waiting. If one is truly waiting, then without their knowing it, the witnessing is worn away. But there is no sense of that until the final dissolution.

Perhaps you find yourself at a bus stop looking at someone who strikes you as especially nervous or impatient. It interests you very much. You simply look, and you observe that the more the nervousness is articulated, the more relaxed you find yourself. When you come more and more to absolute silent observation, you uncover more and more of the observed. At first the observed is emphasized, but your observing faculty is so strong that you are taken by it and you feel yourself in a dimension of stillness that you never experienced before. It is very important.

When observation becomes more and more relaxed and memory does not come in, we really look at something. Then attention automatically unfolds and becomes increasingly without tension. There is no expectation. There is no anticipation. We find ourselves in an observation which is completely dimensionless.

Real observation is a very important faculty which we must learn. Generally, observation is polluted by memory and thoughts, comparison, judging and so on. When the observer remains as the controller, when he looks to take something of the observed, then the observer can never discover itself. Real observation is innocent observation where no one is observing and there is no intention. Observation is welcoming, is openness. In sustaining this openness, open alertness, there is a moment when the energy from the observed, free from all will, from all obtaining, goes back to the observer. Then there is no more eccentric energy. It comes back. I would say it becomes concentric. And when the energy comes back in a concentric movement, then the observer knows itself in the observing faculty. Then there is a feeling of expansion and you live in intelligence and sensitivity.

So the wanting to...the unconscious grasping is really, in essence, a need for power over the object...

Oh, yes.

...which is a mistake almost all disciples make with so-called teachers.

Yes, yes.

Jean, you talked yesterday about security and insecurity. Could you explain it a little more?

The reason you are so conditioned to volitional living, willful living, living with purpose, is because you try to find security. It gives you a false sense of security to project your own experiences and memory and live by these. But you will see that projecting can never give you security. It gives only temporary and apparent security, because life proceeds in a completely other way.

When you give up intentional living, when you are open to life, there is no more place for the person. This openness to life is a perfect insecurity, but in this apparent insecurity for the person there is security. Alan Watts said there is security in insecurity, which means you find your real security when there is no projected security. When you look for security you can never find it, because you project memory, the already known, and life is constantly and completely different from what you expected.

To be attuned to the real nature of life, you must live completely in the unknown, without any strategy. In this attuning, you will find yourself secure. Otherwise, you are swimming upstream all your life. Apparently, the person is in insecurity, but what is not the person is in real security.

When you go on the battlefield you can take all your instruments, all the tools that you need, but you must never codify any way of living. You must be completely open to the moment itself. When you are completely open to the moment itself, there is apparent insecurity, but you will come face to face with real security. We constantly project security through experiences or memory. In projecting security we can never find security. In the non-projecting of security we find real security. But this non-projecting is a kind of insecurity for the person, it is true.

Jean, practically speaking, does this mean no plans, no collecting money, no gathering of things?

I would say: Be alert. Be alert. Simply, be alert. Leave all your luggage at home and be alert. Face life.

Money gives security. Security to pay the bills. I am not talking about comforts or something, but bare necessities. If a situation comes where I see I may not be able to pay the bills even, there is insecurity.

But insecurity is memory. Face the facts. Behave according to the facts. It is the fact which shows you have to act. That is all you can do.

Facts like: the money is running low, should I do something to produce it?

Yes, face what life imposes on you. You do so many things without projecting security or insecurity. When you are thirsty you take a glass and you drink. You do not think about it. There are so many acts in daily life which come completely spontaneously to us according to the situation. But the moment our ego is involved, our sense of person, rightness, what is our due, we are in conflict and cannot act spontaneously. Do not bring in memory.

But Jean, the memory is there. Until it is washed out, it is going to keep on coming. Memory is there from my past, my experiences, my likes, dislikes and so on. When I see an object or run into a situation, a memory comes up to make a judgment of the situation. Somehow that has to be suppressed or it has to be cleaned out. If it is not there at all, it is clean, there is nothing to worry about. But....

What has to be done, do it. Do it because it has asked some action of you. But do not bring in the mind, evaluation, comparison. All that is memory. Face the facts. You will see that the moment you face the facts, you will be solicited to act.

July 17—afternoon

When we emphasize the observer, our consciousness, there is no longer a doer who manipulates the body, who moves the body. There is a completely impersonal approach to the body. All tensions, reactions, even those deeply rooted in the body, have no more hold, and sooner or later this tension is eliminated and we become more aware of the energy body which underlies our physical body. We become familiar with the deep layers of sensitivity of the body and we come to know our original body. But knowing our original body is still more or less a by-product, because what is emphasized is consciousness, our presence.

When we emphasize the feeling sensation, we use our muscles in a different way. Our muscle is in antagonistic function. This means that in this movement there is an agonist and antagonist. In other words, there is one part of the muscle which contracts and the other which expands. When the muscle is wrongly used, there is an over-contraction and an over-stretching, but when we use our muscles with aware feeling, these over-activities are reduced and the muscles, in a certain way, come together and function harmoniously. Then you feel no more hindrance. So the body must become an object of our awareness. When it is felt—allowed to be feeling—it comes to life. This coming to life begins on the level of the skin with tactile sensation. I would say there is a resurrection of the flesh.

I want to clarify further the answer you gave me yesterday. When you say you may receive it, the verb "may" has two meanings: you have permission to, and "may be." But what hinders me receiving it, because up till now I can feel my resistance, my fears, all sorts of emotions? Is it just in my inability to receive, to wait for divine grace to do its work? Or do I still have a role to play?

When I say it may happen, I mean it comes in a certain way like an unexpected gift, when you are open to the unexpected. Then the mind knows there is something beyond it and it is open to a new direction. The mind gives up its determinism. And as the mind gives it up, is open to something unknown.

When you act in your life with will, you will not have any gifts. Few gifts come when willed. But when you are completely open to life, you will be astonished, enriched by the gift-giving. That is why I say you can wish it in a certain form, without willing it.

You mean you can hope for it, but not force it? Can you give it a helping hand?

I will answer it another way. When you are waiting for the expression of life, you are waiting for the gift because all that comes is a gift. The ultimate gift is the waiting.

Waiting for what?

For nothing. It is waiting for its own waiting, waiting without any will. Then this waiting refers to itself. And this waiting is open. You can never take, feel, think this openness. You can never understand it because it is the being understanding. When you say "I have understood," it means the understanding is still a formulation, still a representation. But before you say, "I have understood," there is the living understanding. Later you make it understanding through your formulation, your representation. You must never say, "I have understood." When you "have understood," you represent, objectify, it. Real understanding never says "I have understood." When you are completely in wholeness, it is beyond the mind. Think about it. It is not a specific gift for which you are waiting. The ultimate gift is the waiting itself. Being open. Perceiving.

You said in an earlier book that the aim of meditation in the direct path is the elimination of the object. I wanted to ask you about that. When your awareness is space-like and objects appear within it, coming and going, from that place it seems that one could either go back into dreams with the objects or, if the attention is released somehow, the objects don't appear to be separate. They appear to be one large object. Just one object. Is this the right direction?

Our timeless awareness is the light behind all appearance, all objects. The object appears in this silent awareness and disappears in this silent awareness. So this silent awareness is constantly there. It is a continuum. You do not need to sit in a special way. You can also walk. It is always there. It is there when there is activity and you work, and there when you rest.

But why eliminate the object then? You said that was the most necessary, the final thing. Because you said when the object is eliminated, then the subject is eliminated.

Yes. Because it is the subject which maintains the object. When there is the fusion of the subject in the object, the object has no more hold for its objecivity, and there is no more subject and object. There is only presence. In a certain way the subject and object are superimposed onto our reality. But we are fascinated by the object. It is as when we see ourselves in front of a shop and we look at all the fascinating things—a most interesting computer, one we have never seen before, for example—and we are so taken by this invention that we forget ourselves.

In the end one cannot even speak of "an object." There is only oneness. You can never take consciousness away from the object. But you can take the object from consciousness and consciousness remains. Consciousness just is. It is permanent. Timeless. I have not answered your actual question, but it is answered.

The object is almost an invention of the mind, it seems. In the waiting, it goes away by itself.

The waiting, the essence of waiting is our reality. Because in waiting there is nothing asserted or manipulated or concluded. It also belongs to creative thinking. In creative thinking nothing is asserted, nothing dominates, and nothing is manipulated. It is a simple seeing of the facts. It is a constant interrogation, I would say.

Creative thinking is a constant interrogation. That is why, in a certain way, Krishnamurti speaks of negative thinking and positive thinking. I remember under positive thinking he speaks of scientific thinking, rational thinking. Negative thinking is looking away from thinking. It is thinking which does not start from thinking, thinking which does not start from thought. I never use the terms negative or positive thinking, but he uses them. I thought it might be quite useful for certain people.

The answer came through in what you said. The answer is that the waiting itself is the natural elimination of the object.

Yes.

That is the ultimate negative approach.

Yes. Absolutely. The openness approach.

So the object cannot sprout in the waiting. If waiting is there, the object cannot sprout as an object.

In this openness the object finds its real significance. Only then does it refer to our totality, to our presence. Otherwise, it refers only to an object, our person, and then it is constantly in a relationship of object to object. The person is an object we can know. We know this person who chooses. We know this choice.

If you are in waiting you can't choose. It's impossible.

Yes. Yes. Fundamentally, we know that all is given.

I'm trying to understand, Jean. In the ultimate stillness it seems that obviously the person no longer exists. Is that an egoless state that has to happen before the ultimate awakening? And is that stillness the light that is always constant? Is that beyond consciousness?

When you are completely open there is not a notion of an "I." It is not there. There is also no choice. So what appears, appears anew, but you are not.

July 18

I'd like to go back to the question that was asked the other night about whether the film was already made. You seemed to be saying that there was a destiny, by the fact that you said, "Yes, it was already made." And yet, saying that it was being lived out in timeless space also seems to imply a certain free will.

The film is essentially in the now. But you, as a questioner, are also in the film. The film flows in time. The difference between you and the film is that you are the light that gives reality, existence to the film.

Does this give us the free will of choice?

You have the idea that you act freely. But this acting is also in the film. You are essentially free when you awake in your light.

What does that freedom mean?

Freedom from the idea of being somebody. In other words, the film points to your real nature, which is essentially time-less.

Jean, when you use the word "film," is that synonymous with the idea of objects? It seems to me that...

All that appears is on the film. But you give life to the film.

But if the film is already made and one just gives light to it, it means...?

The word "already" does not apply here. It is constantly in the now. "Already" belongs to time. You create the world the moment you think of it.

Are there five billion individual films, or just one? Does each person have his own film?

His own belongs to what? What belongs to his own? To you? There is no you. There is appearing and disappearing, with which you mistakenly identify yourself instead of identifying with the continuous background, consciousness. There is only a functioning.

The film is functioning?

The film is functioning, without any purpose. So don't emphasize the film; emphasize the light. All that appears is in the film.

It doesn't matter if we're immersed in a mathematical problem or sitting admiring the scenery.

Exactly. All is in the film.

Whether we're global thinking or very self-centered thinking.

You must see what you mean by global thinking. All that appears, all that you qualify as thinkable, is on the film.

Possibly, watching the film without taking part in it is...

You must see what I said, that all you perceive is on the film. But you see very little on the film, because you identify yourself with the film. Because you identify yourself with the film, you see only a certain fraction of it. The moment you really know that you are the light, you will see the film is much richer.

But the watcher of the film is not in the film, is it?

No. The watcher is the light.

Does this light have any identity?

This light is timeless. The film is in time and space. We are here to find our real nature. Take it for granted that it is all in the film, but that you are the light. And I would say, be the light.

The light which makes the film visible.

Absolutely.

The film is readily understandable. It's a mechanical phenomenon.

Absolutely.

One can make cyclotrons and all sorts of things to figure out the various aspects of the film. But it's just all on the film, and it's meaningless.

Yes. But it is something tremendous when you see that what

you are fundamentally is not on the film. It is something…it is a revolution. It is a revolution that makes your mouth immediately fall open. [laughter]

It's a complete mystery.

Yes! It makes you astonished.

Jean, could you say that the welcoming is a bridge between time and timelessness? There is no bridge, of course, but it seems to be the closest to that in the waiting.

Time and space are in the horizontal position, and reality is vertical. There is a moment where the vertical and horizontal meet together. That is in the now. The horizontal can never exist without the vertical. Reality is only in the now, in the present.

Would you say the waiting without waiting is a sort of open-handed invitation to…?

Constantly. I would say you are then in the vertical position. But you must not emphasize the possibility of receiving something, but rather the receiving itself.

The receiving itself. Right. Otherwise I jump into time.

Yes. Yes. The receiving refers to itself. What we call the past, present, and future are only memory. All time, one, two, three, is memory.

Which is the horizontal movement.

Yes. Because what we call present is also the past.

Right.

When there is looking, there is looking. It is only after, that you say, "I looked at the flower, and it was myself looking." But you can never simultaneously see the flower and say that there is looking. Because consciousness itself and its object are one.

So, you're saying the moment is always the vertical.

Always. You can only *be* the seeing. Later you think. You don't know that you think. It is only after the thinking that you can say, "I saw it." But you can be completely aware of the moment. It means you *are* the moment without thinking it. When you think it, it is already the past.

In the moment there is only perceiving, there is only feeling, there is only seeing.

Yes. There is only beingness.

Yes. But it seems like it brings with it a quality of joy.

But in beingness there is no subject-object relationship.

But when beingness refers to itself isn't there a quality of something?

It is beingness. It is impossible to qualify it. When you qualify it, it refers already to the known, to the past. You can't qualify it, you can only say it is a total absence of any need. It is total fullness.

You once said it was "an explosion of wonder."

Yes.

Why is that?

It is an explosion because you have always found yourself in patterns, and suddenly the insight takes you away from the patterns. That is why it appears as an explosion.

In the word "satchitananda" there is the word "ananda", which means bliss. When I look at you, often—especially when I'm at the dinner table and I just look at you—it seems there's just laughter.

There is only looking when you look at me. There is only looking. There is not a looker. And nothing is looked at. No? And then you say, "I looked, and I saw this gentleman."

I feel discouraged because I see patterns repeating and repeating and it's very hard for me to see progress. Instead of feeling freer, I simply feel that these tendencies continually seem to have the same overwhelming strength. And I feel this fear of letting go, the fear of death. I'm very tense. And I'm unable, in meditation, to resolve this, to find free space.

When there is really transmutation, the memory of progress doesn't exist. When you speak of progress, there is comparison. But when there is really transmutation, there is no more comparison possible. It may be that you find yourself in certain situations and you say that two years ago you found yourself in the same situation, but it is absolutely impossible to speak of analogy between your response two years ago and now. You say it is astonishing how I have reacted then, and how I have acted today. I find myself in a situation with more or less the same intensity, the same antagonism, and this time

I feel myself completely free, comfortable. Then you can say, "Yes, I look at things in a different way, and I have made some progress." But as far as your timeless nature is concerned, you can never speak of progress.

But wouldn't there be a feeling of being less victimized by the mind, by tendencies, maybe a greater feeling of distance? I just feel my meditation has not gone deep enough to effect a transformation, and I don't know what to do.

Look at things free from all expectations, without comparison. Then things refer to your presence. That is the only way to come to transmutation. There is no other way to bring real understanding, being the understanding. And in really being the understanding, the intellectual understanding has completely dissolved. Being the understanding means you feel yourself in this totality. Be this totality. Don't be stuck to mind understanding which keeps you in representation.

What is the meaning of "let go," and how to use it properly?

In not letting go, there is anticipation. There is memory and end-gaining.

Not letting go?

Yes. To really face life, you must face it with your openness. So the already known must be given up. You must face life completely open-minded, empty, without any representation. Then you come to the understanding of life, and then you also use life in a right way.

What is the proper way of looking at an illness that one might have, and what is the most effective way to help self-healing?

Our body is mainly felt. The feeling is a global feeling. Every organ in our body is a vibration. All the organs in our body are like a symphony of sounds. When the organ loses its precise vibration, then it is ill. We have already spoken about this. You must stimulate the organ with light vibration. You feel the vibration in colors and sounds. As a treatment, you should visualize certain colors that belong to specific organs, and then bathe in the color, visualize the color in front of you—three or four yards—and go in the color with your energy body, with your sensitivity. You take a bath in the color. Then come back into the physical body, and you will see how the organ reacts after this treatment. The organ which was ill from its tension, tension which belongs to its surroundings, is emptied.

Does one maintain the emptiness?

You must maintain the emptiness. And then again, with this emptiness, bathe in the color. Then the energy body comes back in the physical body, completely refreshed. And you wait to see how this part of your body, which was ill, reacts.

Let's say that you have a cancer growing in your intestine, or something like that. What is the proper attitude to take about that? What do you say to yourself about that? How do you defuse the resistance?

I would say that first it is caused by a lack of certain substances in your body. Or, you can also say there are certain encumbrances in your body, certain wastes that you have not eliminated. So, face the lack of elements in your body and then try to eliminate the waste.

Should there be any intention to heal? Generally you say to live without intention. But when faced with something like that, what should the attitude be?

One must completely surrender to it, in other words, welcome it, accept it, do not refuse it. When you refuse it, then you feed the illness. In other words, you must be positive. You must not refuse it. You must not escape it.

Jean, it seems that if you accept, you create more spaciousness which may create the ability to heal. But what is the difference between acceptance and resignation, which would tend to give a little more negative force to the illness?

When you welcome it, when you take it as a pointer, it is really positive to your illness because then you are not in any way an accomplice to it. You contribute to the healing. Real acceptance is not a sacrifice. There is no resignation, no masochistic element. Acceptance is welcoming. In welcoming it you are completely open to it. There is no resistance, no reaction. In principle, the body comes from health. The body knows its health, because the body has organic memory of the natural, healthy state. Ideally medicine and the doctor help nature. They don't fight the illness. But the specific healing of which we are speaking is that you must completely empty the part which is ill. Then you project this part completely in front of you—not your whole body, only this part. You project it, and then you go in. When you live knowingly in this projection, you are not here, you are there.

Jean, you spoke earlier about living in the sensation of the subtle physical body or the energy body and then coming back to the physical body. I don't quite understand what you mean by that.

You are able to project your energy body in a certain space in front of you. Then you are there, where you project the energy body. You are there, not here. The physical body is here, the energy body is there. You disassociate your vital body from your physical body, your conditioned physical body.

When you say it's there, what is your experience of it?

You are conscious there. You are conscious of the place there, where you project it. You can project an image there, you can sit here and visualize an image. It's not this that I'm speaking of.

Is the projection a sensation?

Yes. Really go there.

How do I do it?

When a mosquito moves in your hair, before you take the initiative to take your hand and explore the place where the mosquito is, you are already there. No? Sometimes you are even too lazy to take your hand and go there. It is enough to think of it, to do it.

So this projection is a thought, in thinking?

You give the order to your vital body to do it.

Jean, could one learn this kind of healing if one were interested, as I am?

Certain books have been written. There are certain hospitals and clinics where you find every room painted a different color, sometimes two colors. There are also rooms with stained glass of different colors.

One uses colors not only for people who are mentally ill, but also physically ill. Because every color has its vibration. This vibration is a physical reality, and it also has its spiritual, psychological expression. You act differently when you see the color red than when you see blue or yellow or violet. You generally look at violet, but you never ask how it acts on you. You may eat a pineapple and ask how the pineapple has acted on you, how your body feels after absorbing the pineapple; but when you inquire how yellow or violet acts on you it's very interesting.

Does everyone respond the same to specific colors or are there differences?

No. It is not subjective. Green or yellow have their expressions. When you sit before a very green meadow and you identify with the green, plunge completely into the green, you will see how the green acts on you; it is very interesting. It needs a certain sensitivity, of course.

Does the energy body have any special significance, or is it just part of the physical body?

The physical body is an extension of the vital body.

So they are both really objects.

Absolutely.

If I sent my energy body to touch your knee, would it be felt?

If you really used the energy body in the right way, it would be felt. And the energy body is not diminished through space.

You might find yourself in Madrid and hear someone in New York. It is very astonishing, but it is true.

In the bodywork, when we're experimenting, looking at a certain posture, how do I know when to come back and when to push it a little bit, to stretch it a little further, not just with the physical body, but with the energy body?

The vital body is the vanguard for the physical body. It goes first and the physical body follows. When a movement is made it must always be made first with the vital body, which then takes the physical body with it. There's a moment when automatically you cannot go further. Then you stop.

If someone is without any particular guidance, doing very intensive pranayama and meditation many hours a day for many months, is there any risk in that, any risk of insanity or energy imbalance in a permanent way?

The moment there is right observation, I would say silent observation, in the silent observation there is inquiring, there is exploration, there is making acquaintance with the perceived, with the object. Then, you can be sure, there is a reorchestration of energy.

I think I have understood that in any situation there is nothing to gain, nothing to lose. Can you clarify that?

When you come to the absolute certitude that what you are fundamentally already is, then there is nothing to gain, nothing to lose, because you are. All kinds of striving, religious overcoming, or what they call knowledge, has nothing to do with what we are looking for. When you really see that there is nothing to lose, nothing to obtain, there is a natural giving up. Then, you really say, "I don't know." In this "I don't know," there is nothing knowable. You cannot project something eventually knowable. You live knowingly in the "I don't know," which is a completely new dimension.

If it is true that there is nothing to gain and nothing to lose and our nature just is, then why take any action? Why not just do nothing?

When you give up all religious longing, you give up all knowledge concerning your real center. Live with this giving up. Don't try to understand it. When you once have seen that there is nothing to obtain, nothing to lose or gain, live with it. All dynamism for obtaining something, for achieving something, all this energy is spontaneously stopped. And what happens then is that it is your experience, your own, your nearest.

Can you speak to us about suffering?

Inquire who is the sufferer. Who suffers? It is the mind which suffers. There is body suffering, but the suffering of which you are speaking is purely psychological. You should explore who is the sufferer, what is the sufferer. You will see that it is only a projection. We are speaking in your case, of course.

It seems that this question is extraordinarily important, about nothing to gain and nothing to lose, because the very thing that seems to alter the openness is the notion that there is something to lose and something to gain. And your answer is very clear. We are looking for happiness and bliss and we always think it's an object. We always want to understand it, read it, think about it, sit and reflect on it. I know that you're right. You demonstrate it every time. But somehow there is a kind of magnetic memory which succeeds in seducing the part of my mind which functions in a system, a belief system, which still works in this pattern. I see the mechanics of it, yet it's like there's something missing. Why does this actually still happen to me now? That's what I don't understand.

When you say there is nothing to gain, nothing to obtain, nothing to lose, is it really your experience that this is so?

No.

It is more or less second-hand information.

Right.

You believe it.

Right.

So, I would say, make it your own experience. All that is attainable, all that you can obtain, you have very often had in your hand, in your profession, and at that moment you were happy—you were in a desireless state. At that moment, there was not a you, an experiencer, nor even a cause of this moment. You were completely one in this happiness. But you also know that you attributed a cause to this timeless moment and that later, the so-called cause that had apparently given you happiness left you completely indifferent. This proves to you that what you are looking for can never be found in something thinkable. That is important. You come to the conclusion that it is the nearest. What is the nearest you can never obtain or lose. It is. It doesn't belong to existence. It is. It is the isness.

In welcoming, I want no more. There is no more wanting, I don't have to change anything.

Exactly. In welcoming you are this fullness, because the welcoming refers to itself.

There is a moment when you say, "What is it? What is life? Who am I?" For the mind, all activity is given up. The moment you give it up there is also some change in your body. All that exists, all that we project, is in front of you, but there is a sudden transference from the front of you to behind. It is the giving up which brings you behind. Because, in a certain way, you feel your reality behind you. All that is in front of you is not you, is an expression of you. It is in space and time. You are behind you. When you give up, in the same moment you are taken behind.

Giving up in this way, and being taken in this way—are they same thing? I mean, is it automatic?

Yes. But you must not dwell on this. Hear it once, and when you have understood, forget it. Don't make a philosophy of it, or a way to approach reality. Of course not.

When you really say, "I don't know," you are free. There is no more representation. You give up. You have looked everywhere, in all directions, and this has brought you to the certitude that it is not there. See how you feel in your body. Your real freedom you feel behind you.

Just as you are speaking now, for the first time I understand experientially the words "being open to openness." Or at least I have the flavor of it. Because I realize the openness I've had before was for the possible knowable, this intriguing phrase you used yesterday. I never thought of it, but I realize that I was being receptive, but waiting for some thing, though I didn't know what it was. And tonight it's clear that openness unfolds from itself unto itself. That the initial psychological acceptance becomes a broader energetic opening that just keeps unfolding from itself. It's quite a remarkable realization.

When the openness refers to itself, there is no more formulation possible. You must be very careful in saying, "I know it." It is a kind of profanity.

I come and I listen to the talks, and I have a kind of general, but somewhat foggy, notion of the way the world is, and the relationship between objects. I've never really taken it as I would a class in mathematics, to understand as a system, because it was my understanding from the teaching that that was not the way to go about it. Is that correct?

When the mind comes to a certain clarity, this clarity is representation. Clear representation is important for the mind. In this representation, the mind knows itself, knows its limits.

Can you speak a little about listening?

Listening?

Yes. We have such difficulties listening to one another.

Real listening is in this openness. But first you should become aware that you don't listen. You can never try to listen. You can never try to listen better. You can only say, "I have become aware that I don't listen." That is enough. Because originally you are listening, originally you are open.

Can you speak on faith in the guru, and detachment from the guru?

You ask a certain question. This question does not come from information from books or from hearsay or from second-hand information. The question comes out from the moment itself. In your absolute earnestness, then, comes the question. "What is life? Who am I? How can I face life? How can I face the expressions of life?" That is your question. Then the teacher gives you certain indications, certain ways how to look and listen. This is second-hand information, too. But you must believe it and make it your own.

You find yourself in New York, and you don't know where to go and you have no map. You ask somebody who appears to knows the streets of New York, because he looks like a New Yorker. So you ask him and he gives you the information on how to go. This is second-hand information, but you must go where he said. You must believe him. And then you will find the street. Then it is first-hand information. In this way you must have faith in the sayings of the guru.

And detachment?

As he gives you the directions on how to find life, how to find your real center, in this moment one cannot even speak of attachment or detachment. There remains friendship, I would say. Friendship.

But the man on the street doesn't feel he's a guru just because he knows where the street is, does he?

In any case, you must accept what he said. Because he has gone the same way. He found it. So he can only say the way that he found, nothing else. You must go the same way.

Without doubting on your way?

You must never doubt the guru. He shows you the way to go. He doesn't go for you; you must go. Then it becomes first-hand information for you. But as long as you have not reached the place or the street, it is still second-hand information. In this connection you must feel a certain freedom, a certain comfort in relation with him. In a certain way he gives you freedom. He doesn't give you any psychological or other holds. You see him, but in reality he is nothing. That is the only way.

When you come here and I say to you, "You are nothing," and you really hear that you are nothing, what happens? There is no more memory. You give up what you believe yourself to be. You find yourself spontaneously in emptiness. But this emptiness is not an object, not a representation. It refers to your totality. It is a global feeling. It is original perception. When you have it once you will be solicited a second time, a third time. But when you have it once, enjoy it!

July 19

Could you speak a little bit about how the breathing is related to the movements?

The posture is one thing, and going into the posture is the second thing. When you go from one posture to another, you must never anticipate. That is living in intention. Once you have given the order to your body to go from one posture to another, you have given the order. But then you remain only in the feeling. You go from one moment to another moment.

There is no anticipation to a finality. And with the breathing it's the same. It means you are completely one with the object which presents itself in the moment. You are completely one with the object, one with your body, one with your body feeling. There is no thinking. There is only feeling. You go with the feeling.

Will you speak a little about resistance. I've been aware in this seminar of my physical resistance and emotional resistance and how they're connected. If you can let go of the emotional resistance, does it release the physical resistance?

The emotional resistance comes up when you relate the posture to yourself.

To the "I," the person?

Yes. You must only function. You have given the order to the body. The body executes the command.

When you find resistance in your body...

Then face the body. Don't face the emotion, face the body. And then come back in the posture, and do it again. But keep the feeling sensation alive, very, very strong. When the old pattern of resistance comes up, don't deal with it, don't fight it, don't control it. What is important is the inner feeling, the inner quality of the body, and your alertness.

But can the resistance you find in your body have an emotional source?

It is the feeling of the body, the resistance, that creates the psychological situation.

Ah.

Not the other way around. In your case, going in front of you, bending forwards, doesn't create a problem. But when you go the other way, there you must be very, very careful. You should really proceed as when you are in a room with no light. You move through touch.

You feel it.

Yes. You really feel it. When there is a reaction, a compensation, come back. Don't relate the bodywork to yourself. You are awareness forever, and there is no "I" to do it, to feel it.

The bodywork is on the observable, the known. It's obvious. We see it. We sense it. Is there ever an action, in the sensible world, which arises from the emptiness?

The emptiness of the body and the mind emptiness are one. Don't make two of them. The body emptiness has its reality, its existence, in your emptiness. When there is really directionless attention, this attention unfolds in intelligence and in sensitivity. When I speak of sensitivity, your body sensitivity is included. You have the impression you don't think with your head, you think with your body. You don't hear with your ears, you hear with your body. You don't smell with your nose, you smell with your body.

The body is the same. Body movement is the same. All appears in your emptiness. All appears in you, but you are not in it. You only know it because it is in you. The knowing capacity is only possible because you are out of what is known. The known must be in the knower. But the knower is not in the known. Otherwise knowing is not possible. The known can never know itself. An object can never know another object.

What is important is that when you come into a room and look around your environment, you look with an open mind. You will be aware when memory comes in, at your office, understanding the problems with which you deal in your business. Refer all those things to your presence, to your globality. Globality means without the split mind, without a mind of choice which lives in complementarity. Don't go into choice. Let the choice come from the situation itself. It is the situation that makes the choice, and you are only the executer of the choice. You are a channel. Perhaps more clearly, you are not the executor, you are the execution. There is no more psychological involvement. This psychological involvement is more or less a defense.

When there is alertness, there is life, it has its own taste—call it love. But there is nobody who loves. You execute things as asked by the situation. You will be astonished at the intelligence that appears when you really look at the facts, not from the point of view of the split mind but from wholeness. The split mind goes into old patterns of like and dislike. But from your totality, from morning to evening you are in a kind of equanimity. It is important. You really live in this equanimity.

I have a question about acceptance. Very often when something has been denied, as when a person finds out someone close has died, there's a sense of pushing that away or wishing it hadn't happened. Then when the realization comes, often there's a grieving. And I wondered if that process of grieving and crying is part of the process of coming to a full acceptance?

I think it is a completely wrong relationship with life.

Wrong?

Yes, wrong. What is important is that you must understand what is life, and what are expressions of life. When you really understand life, dying has a completely new significance. In the West we mainly emphasize the object part. Emphasize life in you, and you will see only life. Face other people and your surroundings with life.

Would you say that dying is a part of life?

Yes. When you really understand life, you can say that every evening you die. Even from moment to moment you die. Your relationship with this transformation is completely different. This understanding gives you a different sleep and waking up.

You say you give yourself to sleep because you know, through memory, that you will wake up tomorrow morning. But there will come a moment when you won't wake up any more. What is important is to know yourself behind the waking and sleeping states. Then there is a completely different approach to the continual changing.

How does the experience of deep, dreamless sleep differ from the sage in the waking state?

You speak of the sage. For the sage the dream state and the waking state are the same. There is no difference. And sleeping is a state, too. These are states which belong to your presence.

Is there a certain self-awareness, a vivid self-awareness or awakeness behind all three?

There is awareness in continuity. And the three states are more or less a superimposition. The moment you are free from any involvement in that waking state, you will also have that distance in the dreaming state.

Just like a phenomenal appearance that's either there or not?

Absolutely. When you dream, it is, for you, a waking state. It becomes a dreaming state when you are in the waking state. You say, "I dreamt. It was a mind production." But it is actually the same. The psychological time may change. In the dream state, in twenty minutes according to your watch in the waking state, you can have three marriages and three or four children. And your children and wife or husband are very beautiful. But it only lasted twenty minutes. [Laughter]

In a situation, a business situation mostly, I get the feeling that

I've been cheated, deceived, or the other party has not lived up to their commitment. For example, they'll say we'll meet for dinner at five o'clock, and the guy doesn't show up. And that's a fact. You said that the answer will come from the situation, but I noticed that the solutions that come to my mind are usually to get even with the party. Is this a healthy approach, or is it something else entirely?

Try for some time to postpone all judgment. Postpone it. When you postpone it you will come back again and look at the fact. Because the reaction is very quick. There is a choice. When there is a choice, don't go in. Try just for one morning. For one morning, try to postpone all decisions. Try to look more deeply.

Let the situation overtake the judging...

Yes. Let the situation come completely to you. Don't judge it. Don't try to take anything from the situation. Wait. Wait till the situation acts really on you. Do it only in the morning. And then you don't do it in the morning; you do it in the afternoon. Become acquainted with this way of dealing with things, with your surroundings. When you postpone judgment, you will have a foretaste of freedom. Because the moment you don't judge or compare, you see facts as they are and you are free from them.

But what happens is, the excitement takes over and I get angry.

That is a fact, too.

In other words, postponing judgment will be postponing function, and postponing action.

Yes. You face the fact. Then you accept the fact. You can only face the fact when you accept it. And then you explore it. But as soon as there is decision, comparison...stop. I would say, for you, postpone it, look at it again.

You receive a letter in the evening. You read the letter and say, "This man is completely impossible." Immediately you react from the letter and take your fountain pen and write a reply. But you don't post the letter in the evening, because you are too tired. Then the next morning before posting the letter you say, "I will look at it again." And you see your reply was completely stupid.

Postpone for the moment. In postponing things, you have the foretaste of freedom. To see the facts, you must accept the facts. In accepting the facts you feel yourself in the acceptance, in your freedom. You are not bound to the situation. You are not stuck to it.

But I have made preparations to meet someone who doesn't show up. This is a fact that he's not at the meeting.

Yes. But that you react is also a fact. That you react immediately and say, "This man is outrageous. I will not deal with him." This is also a fact. The moment you react, see your reaction. And see what is the problem or subject you wanted to discuss. See it again. Suddenly you will discover it is a very good idea that he has cancelled the meeting, because you were not ready to confront him, to face him.

Last night when you were talking about disease, you said that one of the causes of disease could be waste products that are lodged in the body.

Yes.

Could waste products include emotional residue? When you feel anger, for instance, you can find it in your body.

Absolutely.

If it's not processed somehow, can it cause a residual effect?

When you are angry or jealous, all these kinds of qualities that belong to the "I," to the "me," have a very deep reaction in the body. It makes the body red or yellow, they become yellow. Psychological reacting means a deep reaction in the body. The reaction can even go so far as to destroy the body.

So the important thing for physical health is...

It may be that your body has very often suffered through your anger, through your jealousy. And after reacting, you felt your body was not really comfortable. Psychologically you may now be free from the situation, but there is a kind of residue in your body. This residue can perhaps remain for a long time. It can become a pattern. It goes so far that you say, "It is my body." You forget that it was a reaction. But it is still a residue of previous reactions. It means you have disturbed, in a certain way, the rhythms of certain parts of your body. You have disturbed the organic body. So do something to heal your body. There are many forms of medicine which bring you back to real functioning.

You get rid of the residues.

Yes, exactly. In sounds and in colors, as we said, there is a kind of vibration and rhythm. The moment you identify this part with certain elements around you which have this rhythm, it stimulates your rhythm. It is a very fine way to heal. It works for certain people. If it doesn't work, there are many other approaches. There are people who work through acupuncture, and there are certain people who don't react to it. But our psychological behavior acts very deeply on our body.

You see anger come up, and you see as a fact that it's accumulating in the body?

When you see it as a fact you stand out of the process. You are no longer an accomplice to it. As we said yesterday, watch it. Go with it. Sleep with it. Love it. Not only accept it, but become a companion to it, to free it. It is a fact and you must take it as a fact. A fact can only exist when you are completely out of the process. Otherwise it is not a fact. It means seeing things from a completely impersonal point of view, if we can speak of a point of view.

I'm aware of the feeling that I have my life to go back to after this seminar, which is not the way I want to approach it. It's not the kind of thing I want at all. I want this opening, this energy to continue. It just seems beautiful that there's the possibility...that the world isn't really there, or...

But don't go back into the old pattern. Go to your room and see the position of your bed and your writing table and your pictures. Go back and be open to the place where you are living. There are many people who are completely conditioned to the place where they are living. They go away for three weeks to free themselves from habit. Then when they go home they look at it in a new way, so see things in a new way.

And the thing is, without relating it at all to me, you know...

But there is not a "me." [laughter]

Last night when I was rolling up the microphone cord, suddenly there was a déjà vu experience that lasted more than a few seconds. I suddenly had the association of having seen the film twice. I very rarely do that because, of course, I'm not emotionally taken into the film and the actors and all of that. But when I have seen a film twice what becomes interesting is the professionalism of the actors and the props and all the different things around it that make up that particular moment. I feel that my conditioning is to believe that the story and emotion, the fight for free will and all that, is real. That's a deep conditioning. This other is so silent and still, I almost invariably pass it by.

It is very interesting to see a play a second time. The first time you saw it you took pleasure in it, you took something from it. The second time, there is not the slightest intention to take something from it, to learn from it, to have pleasure in it. You simply see it. It is very interesting to see how things appear the second time. Many things come up that you did not see the first time. It's even astonishing to see how much of real value appears the second time simply because you are not involved in it.

Let us have a few minutes of silence.

Mt. Madonna
July-August 1988

———

July 29

In this seminar we emphasize awareness through body sensation. In other words, the body is an object of our attention. What we generally call our body is a contraction, a construction, a pattern. It is conditioned by habit, resistance, memory.

The question is, How can we become free from this conditioning? The body belongs to the five senses, but mainly the body is felt. It is tactile sensation. When our attention is free from intention and tension, the vast palette of body sensations naturally appears. In this body approach we use certain visualizations, for example visualizing space, to come to a body that is completely transparent, completely empty.

We may be aware that when we look into open space our muscles and nerves react in a different way than when we look at a very heavy rock. So to come to the natural feeling of our body we should first visualize empty space and introduce this empty space into our body. We should visualize certain parts of our body and see how this space visualization acts on the muscles and nervous system.

When we face the conditionings in our body we should not stop there. We should first look at the parts of our body which are completely healthy, which are completely empty of aggression, of resistance. From the part that is completely healthy we permeate the unhealthy part until there is a sensation of emptiness in the whole body. In this emptiness the muscles function completely differently. But in emphasizing this visualization, there is no willing. Our attention is completely without any intention, anticipation, end-gaining.

When you say visualization do you mean to use the imagination, the mind's eye, perhaps a joint that is not moving properly, to visualize it as moving with a sense of ease and openness?

The moment you move your lower arm it is the biceps, the agonist, which precedes the movement. But the agonist not only does the movement, it also unnecessarily carries some weight. Generally what happens in our conditioned body is that the agonist contracts through memory and the antagonist relaxes. But when you proceed with the visualization that the body, the arm, is a completely transparent sensation, then you will see the agonist will not contract completely and the antagonist will not lengthen completely. Both will, in a certain way, come together. In coming together they will be completely freed from all tension.

First, you visualize the empty space and you bring the empty space into your body and let it pervade your arm completely. Then you go away from the vision. You remain only with the feeling, with the empty feeling.

So you do visualize with the mind?

Yes, of course. You cannot visualize with anything other than the mind. It is a crutch, a pedagogical crutch. It is a trick, if you like.

When you visualize space and you bring this space nearer to your head you will feel expanded. This expansion is not an idea. You can measure it.

The biceps and triceps function in a new way after you have visualized them. You can prove it. You can measure it.

When you realize you are not your body, does this exercise still help you?

Before saying "I am not the body" you must first know what you are not. Become more and more acquainted with your body. In this way you become detached from your body. There is a feeling of distance.

The moment you become aware of a sensation of your body you are detached from it. In this moment the perceiver is not an object. The perceiver is completely attention. In this attention there is freedom from all expectation. It is a completely innocent presence. At this moment there is no more object to object relationship.

My body experience sometimes seems to be the thoughts or emotions I am feeling.

In this case you have conceptualized the perception. You should free yourself from the concept and only face the perception, the feeling of the body. We can never have a concept and percept together.

Why do you say "visualize space"? It seems to me awareness is space.

Absolutely. But when we speak of visualization we speak only of a trick, a crutch, to free our body from this deep conditioning, heaviness, reaction, resistance, fear and so on.

Of course, the body has its reality in this space, in this reality.

We have identified ourselves with the body. We have become stuck to the body. You may see that when you go to stillness you have a habit of localizing the stillness somewhere in the body and making it a sensation.

In meditation there is no localization. There is no hold on anything. In this total giving up there is no more center.

You have said your emotions are actual changes in sensations in your body. When you visualize your body as empty and non-existent what happens to the existence of emotions? What happens to happiness and anger?

Happiness and anger disappear, in a certain way. They are interdependent counterparts. You cannot have one without the other. When you look at them there is a kind of conversion. Then each of them is unrelated, but remains in your awareness, your attention, your presence.

For healing purposes you can push visualization very far. And not only the visual. You can visualize certain colors that belong to the healing process and you can also produce certain sounds in your body that belong to the healing process.

Happiness, in the ultimate sense, is not a concept. In objectless awareness happiness, which commonly belongs to a psychic experience, is completely reshaped.

The experience of bliss seems to be somewhat body-based. Does that go too?

In real bliss nothing is excluded from the bliss. All is bliss.

For several months I have had almost no energy and something in the throat. I have tried to stay with awareness. But I don't know how to be over a long period of time.

You should visualize this unhealthy part several times in a day. But don't go directly to the unhealthy part. First explore the healthy part. Then you can invade the unhealthy sensation with the healthy sensation. It may not be easy in the beginning.

At first you invade the unhealthy part with the healthy part, later you can visualize the unhealthy part immediately in this space.

So you must visualize several times in a day, until you have adopted a new pattern of sensation. It takes time.

I'm a little confused. It seems the thrust of your teaching is an awareness without choice of whatever happens in the body. If it's a pain or tension that attracts the attention the proper approach is a choiceless awareness of that. But tonight it seems like you're saying, "Don't look right at that, look away, even if you're drawn to that tension, look away to a healthy part of the body and try to visualize spaciousness, and then try to somehow move that spaciousness, without any will power, to invade the healthy part." This is confusing to me.

You are not the body, senses or mind. But in order to be able to say "I am not," you must first know what you are not. So there is a natural accepting of what you are not. In this accepting there is not an "I" that reacts, controls. It is simply attention.

You will see the conditioning of the body is very strong. That means the patterns are very deep. So you go to many levels of the body feeling. All these levels, you are not. Still you must know what they are, until you come to the absolute natural feeling of emptiness. Then when you close your eyes and try to visualize your body, you will not find it. It is expanded in space.

There may apparently be a contradiction. But there is actually no contradiction.

Evil or negativity seems to have its own existence. We can choose to invite it into our lives, accept it, or not have it present.

Evil for whom?

Obviously, evil for the person overwhelmed by self-doubt, negativity, etc.

It refers mainly to the "I." In the absence of the "I," the "me," there is no more inner accomplice to the emotion, what you call evil. There is no more inner accomplice with feelings. They disappear.

It is not the evil we must face, but we must see from which point of view we are looking. When we look from choiceless awareness, directionless attention, our point of view is openness. It is in this openness that all will be explained. It explains itself.

When the body becomes part of our objective awareness there is a time when the body truly lives in our awareness and the emptiness of our body belongs to ultimate peace.

Is it effective to just drop the idea of someone trying to gain clarity, to just be in the sensation of the moment, to give no importance to the mind?

When you know yourself in this objective awareness, multidimensional attention, things and people appear to you in a different way. You don't see them any more from the point of view of your personality, but you see them from your transpersonality. You don't impose any pattern on them. You simply listen to movements, to the speaking, to the formulation. You listen. In this listening to the other person there is love. In a certain way you also stimulate the other person. The person feels himself free. There is no more superimposition of the personality. Then there is no more object-object relationship.

Are you suggesting we live freely in the openness?

We generally call it pure perception, direct perception. In direct perception the mind doesn't control, interpret, bring in the past.

In the beginning there is the perceived and the perceiver. Of course what we call perceived and perceiver is mind. But there comes a fusion where there is no more perceiver, no more perceived, there is only perceiving and perceiving is being.

Then you live totally your complete freedom.

You drive your car according to the road and the other cars. You function according to the situation. All that appears lives in your freedom.

This kind of awareness could be done with any object. Is the reason we are doing it with the body because the ingrained habits are so deep and this is a way of cleaning them out?

Yes. There may seem to be a little contradiction. We often speak of the direct approach, but here we are taking pieces of the progressive approach.

U.G. Krishnamurti, not J. Krishnamurti, says a whole different thing happens in the body when the universal life energy moves through the body, and any awareness, any letting go, is futile.

You must make the distinction between pathological appearance and the changing of the body, when spontaneously the notion to be this or that disappears and you see life from your wholeness. In this spontaneous change there is some other brain function. So one may feel physiological change, but it is not the process mentioned by U.G. Krishnamurti. This man is a pathological case.

You spoke about direct perception. I notice that sometimes the personality jumps in and prevents a direct perception.

Yes. It is a reflex deep-rooted in us. We go directly from cognition to recognition.

This uprooting of our conditioning, is it instantaneous, not a progressive process?

In the direct approach one points directly to the Self, to the ultimate. All belongs to the choiceless awareness. In the progressive way you remain in the subject-object relationship. At the end you may find that you can never free yourself from this subject-object relationship. Choiceless awareness, attention, is non-dual. There's nobody to be aware. There's nothing to be aware of. There is only awareness.

We sometimes use elements that belong to the progressive way. Body awareness, for example, belongs, in a certain way, to the progressive way. But here we emphasize the attention. The moment we listen to our body we make our body completely free from repetition. In this moment the attention refers to itself. You know in the moment itself that you are attentive.

So evil and negativity serve as an object to bring us back to our awareness?

The object, in a certain way, brings us back. It may also be an accidental object like illness or beauty.

Do you believe there are actually accidents?

No. The mind, the ego, believes in them. It is only an idea to maintain somebody. If you believe in accident you also believe in non-accident.

Is "dying to the body and being reborn to the spirit" another way of saying what you are saying?

The teaching mainly concerns the dying of the "I," the "me"; then you are free from psychological memory.

Can this shift happen without crisis, or is crisis an element of it?

In principle, there are no crises. But practically speaking there are crises.

Practically speaking, can there be a non-crisis jump?

Crisis belongs to the psyche. It is like a spiral. It goes up and it goes down. When it goes down there are moments of non-crisis.

As a doctor you intervene in those moments when there is no crisis because in the moments of non-crisis the patient can prepare himself for the crisis—how to approach the crisis in a different way.

It seems to me that the crisis is associated with the letting go of the "I," and it can be a struggle, an emotional upheaval. Is this a necessary component?

As soon as the conditioned mechanism has no more role to play, there is an up-giving and in this letting go there is pain, so-called pain.

Some people have described enormous crises, they have come to the brink of losing their sanity, have been unable to take care of their body functions for weeks or months during this transition. Is this a necessary component?

We must be very careful when we look at them. There is the pathological case and there is a normal transformation.

There was a big crisis in St. John. Also Ramakrishna. But you must be very careful...There may be a touch of the pathological.

This pathological reaction is really a reaction. It is a refusal. In normal transformation there is no refusal. There is suffering in a certain way, but this suffering is of a completely different quality.

Why do you teach?

There is nobody who teaches. There is only teaching. In reality there is no teaching because there is nothing to teach.

How can one be free from psychological memory?

The moment the reflex to be an individual entity dies you live in the present, from moment to moment.

You go back to the past because you have learned certain things from the past. This we call functional memory. But you don't go back to the past to retain the "I," the "me." Generally our daydreaming, our thinking, is from past to future. We are living in a becoming process. We believe we are something.

It is quite beautiful when you live in the present. Memory is there, but not psychological memory, not the desire to be somebody. You have moments in daily life when you are so, when you don't go back to the past, you don't create the future. You know these moments.

July 30

Could you speak about the role of truth-telling as it affects the realization of our true nature?

What do you understand by "truth?" You must first discover what is untruth. What has no existence in itself is untruth, it needs an ultimate knower, consciousness. When you have really discovered this untruth you will find yourself in being truth. You can always objectify untruth but truth can never be objectified. You are it. So the moment you have really discovered what is untruth, you find yourself spontaneously in truth. From this point of view you will see there's no untruth, there's only the extension of truth. It is more or less an expression of truth.

But never try to objectify truth, to localize it. Never. Truth is in your absolute absence, when *you* are completely absent.

It makes it sound as if almost any action would be justifiable if it is an extension of truth.

When action springs from non-action, then it springs from truth. When action springs from action it is reaction.

Since being with you I've had a sense of coming home and there's a real sense of peace. But with that is the feeling of wanting to be affirmed or acknowledged by you. I look at that and ask "Who's wanting to be affirmed?" and although it's subsiding it still arises again and again. So my question is: Where is the place for me to be affirmed by you, the teacher, the guru? And is it one more mistake of the arising of the ego?

Who looks for affirmation? Who? When you live really in this homeground, the homeground doesn't look for anything. You have had a glimpse of what we call truth. Be completely attuned to this glimpse. You have it. You need only to be established in it. So live with it completely. It looks for you. Looking for affirmation, recognition, is more or less a going away from it.

It's difficult to formulate the question, but I'll start with my experience. Normally, I'm asleep. That is, I'm in fantasy, in the mind, not in perception, so that I'll be walking in beautiful woods but thinking about something else. But something wakes me up and I come back to where I am. This awareness that brings me back to where I am makes me ask, "Who am I? Am I the mind? Or is the mind only looking at the mind?" I can look at feelings and sensations in the body because they are objects, but who is looking? Do I make any sense to you?

The question is, "Who am I?" [laughter]

But it's important to feel who I am. It's disturbing to go back and there's just nothing there! But still there is. That's the dichotomy: There's nothing but there's something, and that makes me suffer. The more I look, the more it hurts. I know the hurt is a fantasy too! All this goes on inside of me and I would like to comprehend it. The effort to comprehend is maybe wasted energy in a way. I never will...

When you ask the question "Who am I?" you have no reference to the already known, you live automatically, spontaneously, in the unknown. It is in this moment when there's no
reference to the already known that the "I am" appears. But
the "I am" is never named, never pronounced. The "I am,"
when you speak it, is a form of assertion. But the "I am" springs
up when you say "I don't know" and there's no reference to
something knowable, when there is an absolute "don't know."
Then the "I am" takes you. But it's not an affirmation, not an
assertion, it is an absolutely global feeling of certitude. All
else—what you perceive, what appears—is mind. The waking
state, dreaming state, sleeping state appear in mind. But you
are not the mind, you are the knower of the mind.

*How can you know without reference? How can you know without
knowing something?*

"I know" and "I don't know" are both concepts appearing in
the mind. When you see it clearly then there is a convergence
of "I know" and "I don't know," and this moment reveals the
"I am," which is beyond knowable and not knowable.

Right now my perception is: "I am."

Perception belongs to the "I am." The "I am" is behind all
perceptions. It gives light to the perception. But it cannot be
perceived.

*So in my sitting here right now, I'm not entirely in a dream, there's
something real?*

Perhaps it would be good for you to inquire what is the motive
of your suffering. Listen to this suffering. It may be a pointer.
Suffering is always a pointer. To listen you must be still;

otherwise, you cannot listen. In this listening there's no affirmation, no assertion, there's only openness. And when the listening is open the openness appears as "I am," but you can never think it or assert it. It is an eternal question, an eternal waiting.

I think I understand, thank you.

In the last year I've entered into two peculiar states, or non-states. There's absolutely no problem but something needs clarification. There is a great deal of energy that's shooting through the body. This morning I lost the body, although it's so vivid.... Emotions come up, they're all ok, they're just there. And yet there's a fear because things occur and I have no control.

But do not control. Why are you looking for control? Watch only. Listen to it. Be witness to it. In witnessing there's no controller.

What if I'm teaching and a great laughter comes up, or I'm walking down the street and start crying? Normally, there's a social convention that controls these happenings, but if there's no controller and it just comes up and it's really ok....

Watch it, just look at it.

There's nobody there to watch it. There's just some kind of confusion in it that needs clarification and if there's a problem it's that energy...it's the fear...there's a sadness. It's very lonely.

Do not interfere. Do not control. Let it happen. You'll see that you do not let it happen, you interfere. You direct it, control it. You never face the actual sensation, the perception. Let the sensation be an object of your awareness and you will feel

132

some space between the object and the observer. You will no longer be so involved.

So there's no proper position relative to this energy? Because it's hard to walk sometimes, hard to function, hard to pick up a fork because there's so much energy....

When you simply watch this energy, it comes to a reorchestration, an integration. But when you don't watch it, when you control it, think about it, analyze it; when you interfere, then there is distortion.

Someone said once that to be unable to stay present to what you're experiencing is to give your true power away. Would you say witnessing is the ability to stay present with what you are witnessing?

As long as there is an "I," a "me," a self, there is witnessing. When you recognize that this self is an illusion, an appearing in mind, an object like any other, the reflex to be someone disappears and with it, the witness.

But the witness is an important stage...?

Yes. It is a crutch, a very important pedagogical crutch to bring you to know you are not the doer, not the thinker, you are the witness. In saying I am the witness you don't go any more into the recording: "I am the doer, I am the thinker, I am the enjoyer, I am the sufferer." There's only function.

What is the significance and the importance of this state?

You mean the state of the witness?

133

The state of the witness, when there's no mind, no memory, only perception, no concepts.

The Ultimate Witness where one can no longer speak of a witness is the "I am," pure consciousness.

Does the significance lie in the "I am" state itself or in what it does to you? Is it significant because you feel completely free, one with the universe or God? Is the feeling it gives you important or is it important because it is the truth?

When you are established in truth you live your autonomy; in other words, you are free, free from what you are not. You are a happy being. But at the end when you look deeper at all your motives, you look for happiness and very often you may have these moments of happiness. But after these moments the "I," the "me," appropriates them for itself and makes them psychological. Psychological happiness has nothing to do with ultimate happiness, this ultimate happiness where no one is happy and there's no cause of the happiness. It is completely causeless.

One could almost think that an infant might have that kind of happiness and that the mind has developed memories and psychological complications which can be dropped when it realizes it. The fact that we can drop all this does not prove for me that even this does not belong to the mind. If all belongs to the mind and the mind realizes this, it may still be all in the mind. Is it just the other side of the coin or is it universal enlightenment?

All this belongs also to the mind.

Does happiness belong to the mind also?

The mind belongs to happiness but happiness does not belong to the mind.

A child is born out of happiness. It first appropriates itself to its environment in the mother and when it is free from the mother it appropriates itself to its other environment. There's a moment when the happiness identifies itself with the object and then you lose the happiness.

When the "you" in you becomes happy, you lose happiness.

Exactly, you make an idea of happiness, then you lose it. Because in creating psychological happiness we veil the real happiness.

It seems that there are many masters who have experienced the "I am," but very few have become established in it. Can you speak about this?

You must first have a glimpse of this permanent state, then this glimpse, in a certain way, looks for you. When you have the glimpse once you'll have it very often—between two thoughts, between two activities, before going to sleep or waking up—until you are established, until you are it in non-action and in action. But make sure it's not in the mind. Don't look for it in the realm of the mind.

You asked yesterday if there's a teacher. I told you there's no teacher, no teaching, nothing to teach. There's only being open to the openness. It was not striking enough for you. If we would live in another century I'd say we'd close the shop because there's nothing to sell and nothing to buy. [laughter]

I wanted to ask you about the exercises. What can I do about falling asleep during the exercises?

What is important is that you slept well. [laughter]

What about spacing out, daydreaming, during the exercises?

It may be an adequate moment to discover the dreamer. Once we have discovered the dreamer there is no more going away and all the energy that was directed in the becoming process refers to the moment itself. And then there is a stop. Be completely attuned to the stop.

But this habit of daydreaming not only appears when you do the exercises or other activities. Anticipation is daydreaming. Our aspirations and goals are daydreaming. There's a tremendous energy wasted in this end-gaining where we are looking for survival, survival of the "me," the "I." This energy is useful for discovering what we are not and revealing what we are fundamentally.

Earlier you spoke about the light behind all perceptions and in one of your books you spoke of being visited by a light which your teacher explained as light reflected by the self. Would you talk about this light? Is it the pinpoint of light that appears when you close your eyes, or is it the clearness of things, or something else?

When you come to the point that you really see that there is nothing to be taught, nothing to become, to attain, then you are free from all expectation, all dynamism to produce. It is a normal, spontaneous stillness. You are open to what you are and the presence that you call a teacher is knowingly established. Poetically speaking, it is a transmission of the flame but there is nothing transmitted. Transmission is only a way of speaking. You are stimulated.

You live mainly in a landscape furnished with many objects. You are attracted by all the objects, but in this attraction you completely lose the sense of space. When we speak of light it means that there is an absence of all representation. When you do not project an absence of consciousness onto the absence of objects, you will suddenly feel yourself in a completely new dimension of space.

Enlightenment is only the moment when there's the absolute understanding that what you call the "me," the "I" is nothing other than a fabrication of the mind. This understanding is the freeing of the mind, the freeing of the self, and you feel yourself in openness, in this not-knowing.

Is any life situation workable? For example, you say to be the witness, but in my experience some life situations are so full of demands and activity that it's very hard to create the space for that kind of awareness. Should one change one's life in any way, or go on retreats where there is the time to have some glimpse of the non-state which then alters one's life, or is every situation workable?

You know only relationship where you take yourself for somebody, that means for an object. When you take yourself for somebody you see only objects, so in this relationship you are completely stuck to the other "object." There is no space feeling, there is constantly invasion of your space. This absence of space-feeling is familiar to you. But you also know relationship when the "I," the "me," has no role to play, as it is sometimes in love.

It is only in the absence of the "I" that there is space-feeling relationship. There's no dynamism to grasp, to take, no "I want." Become more aware of these two states.

But the pattern of taking oneself for an object is so strong it seems to be linked to survival. If I don't hold onto me, I won't survive.

It is very deep-rooted. You can never produce the dying. The only thing is to see that you have enclosed yourself in a world of objects. In your question I see you would like to try to get out of the world of concepts. But your "I," your "me," belongs to this concept, so you have found books and you have certainly listened to many teachers, and one has given you many tricks, ways to come out of this conceptual universe. But in reality you turn in a vicious circle. When you really see it, you will already be out of it.

July 31

In order to attain liberation is it necessary to go through yoga or some physical disciplines, or is it enough to be in the presence of a master?

Ask yourself first, "Who is it who is looking for liberation, who finds himself in bondage?" In that question you will find the answer. You will see there is nothing. There is nobody.

You project somebody to be liberated, somebody in bondage. This somebody is an object among other objects. See very clearly there is nobody to be liberated, nobody is in bondage.

When we do breathing exercises you talk about the gap at the end of exhalation....

The underlying reality of the activity of breathing is the truth; it is what you are fundamentally. The inhalation and exhalation are more or less superimposed on this reality. So when you take the gaps in breathing as an absence of activity then you miss the presence, you miss the truth. This gap can never become an object. You are completely one with it. It is a non-dual moment—if we can call it a moment—where there is no subject-object relationship.

The breathing exercises here are not taken as in the Yoga system. In the Yoga system they are more or less a technique for directing certain energies in our body. Here the breathing exercises—if we can still call them exercises—are for a spiritual purpose.

When we are trying to feel the whole body in a posture I go back and forth between visualizing and feeling.

You cannot project a picture at the same time as there is something heard, something touched, something smelled. You can never have them together. So you should first visualize the picture, the empty space. Transpose this empty space into your body. You will see immediately how this picture acts on you. And then you go away from the picture and there is only sensation.

In sensation there is no representation. No thinking. No concept. Only your moment-to-moment being. It is like when you walk through the streets without the idea of going anywhere. There is no anticipation and no finality.

When you say, "Feel the entire structure of the pose as an architect," do you let it come to you, or do you try to see it like a drawing on a page?

You should be able to visualize, to project the physical body in front of you. Then completely go into this projection with all your vitality, your energy, so that you are one with it. If, in this projected energy body, you make an invisible movement you may feel some muscle reaction, that is, memory, in your static, physical body. So you must completely detach the projected fluidic energy body, full of sensation, from the static physical body. Detach the invisible movement from the old muscle-structure. When the sensation is completely detached from the old physical body, it will take the physical part in charge. So first see yourself in space, then live completely in this space.

What is the purpose of doing these exercises?

It is a pastime. We must have a reason to be together. Are you satisfied? [laughter]

I have this idea that you and I live in different worlds. In my world I am still a body and there are separate objects. I know that you tell me it is an illusion. But how much of an illusion? If a bomb dropped on us and we were all turned to dust, would that have any effect in your world?

In your world there is fear. There is anxiety. There is lack of freedom. Explore your world. Explore it. Don't judge it. Don't make any interpretation, any conclusion. Explore it. Then one day you will find yourself beyond the explorer.

You don't know what an illusion is. You've heard of it. You've read about it. When you explore, see how the exploration acts on you. That is important.

How this reaction, this action, acts on you is the turning point.

You speak often of glimpses of reality. In the last couple of days I've had such glimpses. Is there nothing I can do to extend those times?

There is nothing to do. In doing, you go away from it. See it. Discover yourself in the seeing. The seeing is the answer. It is what you are looking for.

Emphasize the seeing. Seeing is stillness. Nothing is seen. You are more or less looking for a state, an object. But what you are can never be objectified.

Be completely open to your surroundings. All your surroundings are objects. Surroundings begin with your body, senses and mind. And your further surroundings are body, senses and mind, too. All is object. You are the ultimate subject. The ultimate subject can never be objectified. All that exists, all that is perceived, are objects in your awareness.

So be completely open, until one day you discover yourself in this openness. You can never assert it. It is a non-state where you are constantly in question. You will see that this question is the answer.

I watch holding on and desiring, and repeating pattern after pattern. I'm wondering, what is letting go without trying to force it?

When you look at the patterns you are out of the process. When you look at them you are completely detached. Then turn your head. Look to the looker. You will never find the looker, because you are the looker.

It will seem obscure for you. But think about it, tomorrow.

You tell us the various characteristics of this state, how you have felt, etc. So the mind has a tendency to compare, "Am I experiencing this...?" Is it possible to be in that state and not know I am in it?

But you can never know because there is not a knower. The knower belongs to knowledge. Knowledge belongs to the mind.

So the second question is if you are in it, is it possible that you can't even say what it is, only live it?

You can only live it. You can never know it, because it doesn't belong to the mind. It is the mind which asks the question.

Have you ever had an experience where you sat there with all the students and had nothing to say?

In reality there is nothing to say. We are here only for the joy of being together.

What you are looking for, you can have. You can have it now. But in a certain way you refuse it. You can only have it in one moment, in one instant. That is why I call it apperception. If you look for it in progression you remain in the mind. You may live in many interesting experiences but you remain in fear. You can have it only in an instant. Then, when you look at yourself, you will no longer find the pattern to which you are accustomed.

It is like an ant looking for its house, which you have crushed with your foot. You will find that for some time it is uncomfortable because you can no longer find your pattern. It is very interesting because there is no more suffering. Automatically, your conceptual world comes to you in another way. The brain will function in a different way and this change may at first cause little physical disturbances. But the real transmutation of the mind is only from this point. Other transmutations are only changing the furniture; facing the bed south and then facing it north.

One asks you to look at the body without judging it, without comparison, without interpretation, without conclusion. Only listen. Look into it. Listen to the body without asking. In this listening, this looking, there is no role for the "I," the "me."

Earlier you spoke of the body movements and postures as a pastime, a pretense to come together.

You must grasp it immediately or forget it. You are laughing three days after the joke.

Why is it that so few people throughout history have experienced this transmutation? Is it an evolutionary step?

Who asks the question? Is the question not asked for psychological survival?

When I'm observing my mind and it is preoccupied with an earlier event, it seems like there is something making that mind go round and round.

The past has only one value: not to repeat the error. But it has no value which belongs to the moment itself. So you may learn from your past, but don't build the future with the past.

You said the world of illusion is characterized by fear and anxiety. In the world you live in is there ever a situation where fear could arise?

Only an object can experience fear. If you identify yourself with an object, then there is fear. As long as you believe yourself to be somebody there is fear and anxiety. As an object you live in insecurity. To maintain what you think yourself to be, you try all means to be free from fear and anxiety, but you find yourself in a vicious circle. One day you will see the person is only a mind construction made up by memory, education, experience, society. It is only in this moment that you become free from fear and anxiety, because then you no longer need to preserve this I-image. You see that it has no reality.

What about biological fear?

When you look at the world, your surroundings, from the point of view of what you believe to be, there is fear. When you look at the world from your totality, which is no longer a point of view, there is no longer fear.

When there is fear, first free yourself from the concept of

fear and then face the perception. And then ask, "Who is afraid? Who has fear?" In asking the question you objectify, distance yourself, from the perception. So the moment fear appears, free yourself from the concept and face the perception.

When one does not identify oneself as an object, are there objects in his world? A watch remains a watch and you can see what time it is, but you see it in a different way. You don't see it as separate. You see it as a reflection of awareness.

Exactly! The scientist believes that an object has an independent existence. When you go deeper, you see that an object cannot exist without awareness.

When you live in globality you are no longer bound to the objects, no longer bound to your surroundings. The objects belong to you. In a certain way they are in you. But you are not in them.

You say this stage is not progressive, that you arrive immediately. Do you mean to say that the first moment you found yourself in it, it had all its ramifications and subsequently no other experiences were added to it?

When you have this sudden insight and you look at your surroundings, your surroundings appear differently because the patterns you have created in you are the patterns created by the mind, the "me," the "I." These patterns are only for security for the "I," the "me." But the moment you have this sudden insight these patterns become only a kind of grimace.

Does this state have its own characteristics? Are there different types of experience in that state that you are now open to?

In this non-state an experience appears temporarily. Every experience appears in non-experience. The real experience is non-experience. If you remain an experiencer you remain in the garage. A real experience must dissolve in non-experience.

When you have this sudden insight it strikes all your psychosomatic being. It leaves an echo in this psychosomatic being. This echo is a reminder. That is enough.

Do you think we will all have this insight you speak of?

Of course. You cannot be one moment without it. You *are* it.

So what is it that we are waiting for?

You are only accustomed to relating to objects, so you wait for something, but what you are fundamentally is not something. When you really wait for nothing, you are open. You will find yourself in the open waiting, not in waiting for something. Then you will see that what you are waiting for is the waiting without waiting, the openness.

Does this waiting take energy?

As long as there is directed energy in this waiting, there is projecting, there is waiting for something.

This waiting is completely free from all projecting. In this waiting there is no expectation. When you say really profoundly, "I don't know," in this not-knowing there is no longer any reference. When there is no more reference, all dynamism is stopped. So there is no longer anything eccentric. All energy that has been explored in an eccentric way becomes concentric. It is an absolute state of waiting, which is space; there is no center, no frontier. It is an empty space. It is the ultimate receptivity. You can also call it intelligence but there is nobody who is intelligent. There is only presence.

There is nobody to look for something, because it is your nearness. Nothing can be more near to you than what you are. It is enough to live with this for some time, not to think about it, not to manipulate it, but simply to live with it.

It seems initially as though the thinking mind is everything, but when there is awareness the mind is seen in different ways. What is the mind when it is used properly?

When you live in openness the mind is only function. From the point of view of awareness the mind is a vehicle.

A vehicle for communication?

For many things. The mind lives in awareness, there is function but nobody is functioning. There is not a functioner, not a doer. There is only function. In painting there is not a painter. There is only painting. When there is a painter there is no longer painting.

August 1

It seems as though thoughts appear from somewhere deep inside and come to the surface. Is there a belief that keeps the process happening?

I don't give you exactly the answer to your question. The energy which you need to be, this energy comes directly from being itself. This energy must not be dispersed. It is only for the Ultimate. When you know that what you are fundamentally can never be objectified, can never be an object, there is no more dispersion of energy to look for something objective, perceptible.

If I give an answer to your question it belongs still to the dispersion of your energy. Do not misunderstand, I speak of spiritual energy which comes directly from the Self.

Is that when the reorchestration of the energies, that you talk about so often, happens?

Yes, when this energy is used for something else, it is dispersion. There may be on the body level a kind of energy. I do not speak of this energy. I speak only of what comes directly from what you most desire.

Are you saying there are two kinds of energy?

There is only one energy, of course, but this energy of which I speak comes *directly* from what you desire.

It takes a certain discrimination to use energy. We come to using it rightly through inquiry. Inquiry frees you from dispersion.

Does inquiring mean loving what you are inquiring about?

In inquiring you welcome all the facts in your life. In this inquiring, choosing does not come in. Welcoming comes from your completeness, your totality. In this completeness there is no division, no positive, negative, pleasant, unpleasant. So you see things as they really are, as facts. It is only through welcoming them that there is right acting.

When I welcome anxiety or fear, I experience a reduction of the anxiety. Then I want more of the reduction, then I get lost.

When you become more and more accustomed to welcoming there are times when you no longer emphasize what you welcome. You emphasize the welcoming itself. And this welcoming is not objective. You cannot think it, feel it, localize it, because you *are* it.

Anxiety and fear arise only when there is object-to-object relationship. In your fullness, in this welcoming, there is no fear. And when fear comes up, free yourself from the concept fear and look at the perception. When you also welcome the perception there is no accomplice to it and it dissolves. Then ask again the question, "Who has fear?" because only an object can have fear. A subject cannot have fear.

This teaching seems to emphasize the non-personal. What happens when I go back into the world, how can I deal with the people I work with, live with, and so on?

You cannot deal with your surroundings according to certain systems or ideas. There's nothing codified on how to deal with this question. You must see it and deal with it in the living moment itself. The real answer is to be it, to live it. Otherwise it is more or less an intellectual communication. If it is with your patients, let them express themselves completely. Don't interfere. If you see he has forgotten something in his explanation you must tell him that he forgot something. He must completely empty himself. When he is completely empty, there is the answer. Perhaps not the formulated answer, but the real answer, the living answer.

The patient tells you what happens in his life, this is more or less self-memory, of course. And at these moments when the patient speaks to you, in a certain way he objectifies, he pictures, what he tells you. And he feels himself at a certain distance. He questions himself, he questions his memory. This distance is important. In looking at what he communicates to you he finds himself in a certain welcoming. He may have a glimpse of the real living answer. He will feel a certain comfort after telling you what he has to communicate.

What does one do when an emotion seems to be overwhelming?

When you are completely identified with your emotivity you cannot do anything. It is only after the crisis that you can do something. Then, objectify your emotivity. Feel where it is localized in certain levels of your body. When you localize it, it no longer has a hold because you, as observer, have a distance from the emotivity and it dissolves. Then go back again and ask the question, "From which mechanism does this reaction come?" because emotivity is a reaction. You will see that this emotivity is a reaction that belongs to a kind of hypothetical person. This you must see.

You will first be aware of it after the emotivity. Later you will be aware during, or even before the emotion comes up. But the moment you feel reaction in you, immediately objectify the reaction. Don't wait and let it take hold. The only thing is to free yourself from what you believe yourself to be.

It seems that we are always creating dualism, which dissolves in witnessing.

The reaction takes place in object-object relationship. The moment you become aware of it, you are completely out of the process of this object-object relationship.

Would you say more about dispersing energy, conserving energy, and using it in different ways?

The energy of which you are speaking comes from what you desire. What you really desire comes out of discrimination. You must see very clearly that what you desire can never be on the objective plane. An object apparently gives you, for a certain moment, satisfaction. But at the moment of living the happiness, the joy, the object, the so-called cause of this happiness, is not present. And also the you that you believe to be is not present. There is only happiness. It is only afterwards that the ego, which has been struck by it, says this happiness comes from this circumstance, or this person, or this object.

This you must really see—that there is no permanent happiness in objects. And then you will live in a happiness where there is no one who is happy, there is only happiness. You will feel this in discrimination, in inquiring, in certain moments in your life. But you are constantly in striving, in accumulation, competition, end-gaining, becoming.

When you live constantly in the becoming process, at the end there comes the question, "Is what I am looking for *really*

objective?" and you will see that the many things that prom-
ised you happiness one or two years ago, now leave you
completely indifferent. You can never attain in the objective
world, in the perceived world, what you really desire. When
you realize this, there is a stop. There is a stop because there
is nothing further to inquire.

But then there comes the desire for this desireless state.
From this moment there is a different orchestration. You no
longer spend your energy on things that have no value to you.
You spend your energy on things that glorify the ultimate.
There are still a certain number of objects in our world that
glorify the ultimate! So, in this way, your energy is no longer
dispersed, it is concentrated, it is oriented. The energy to attain
this desireless state, this permanent happiness, comes from
the permanent happiness itself.

Of course, all that is perceived is energy: energy, matter
and movement. There may be a kind of hierarchy of energy.
This I don't know. For me, all is energy. But this spiritualized
energy is a particular energy. It comes directly from what you
most deeply desire.

In inquiring, this spiritual desire comes up. It's only in
welcoming your surroundings that there is understanding.
There is no one who selects; selection comes when you
welcome things.

The understanding comes directly from what you welcome. Because the solution is in the environment, not in you.

*I experience anxiety and fear, and when I'm sensitive to who is
experiencing these sensations I can disperse them. As they disappear, a certain energy seems to be created because I'm liberated
from the hold they have on me.*

In understanding all your motives and actions there is discrimination. In this discrimination you use the energy in the

right way. It is a kind of selection, but *you* don't select it. The selection comes directly from what you observe.

You know that you utilize your energy now differently than you did twenty years ago. You were interested in so many things twenty years ago that you are now indifferent to. It takes a certain maturity to visualize energy in the right way.

I don't understand what you mean when you say energy comes from desire.

When you desire to be what you really are, that comes from your being itself. It is very strong. That's why I often say the Self is looking for the Self. It is the Self in you that is looking for the Self. These Selves are not two. It is the same Self.

In psychological theory there's a lot of emphasis placed on the mourning, the grieving process. Is this contrary to the teaching that there is no real "me" to grieve?

When there is relationship with others, and this relationship is based on love there is no emotivity. There is not a you and not another. The emotivity that disturbs you is when there is object-to-object relationship.

Should one mourn the absence of a teacher?

There is not a teacher and not a pupil. There is only friendliness. There can't be emotivity, for any emotivity hinders you from being. There is only teaching. Free yourself from the teacher and the pupil.

See that your relationship is from object to object. Take note of it. Realize that very often you take yourself for Joseph Smith. All these years you have taken yourself to be Joseph Smith. All that you have accumulated is Joseph Smith's. There is only looking for security for Joseph Smith. When you see it really clearly, it appears as an enormous nonsense in your life. This seeing will strike you so strongly it has an effect on you. You feel it in the body.

Give up Joseph Smith! Joseph Smith has no existence; he is memory, accumulated memory, society, education, experience, and so on. Don't deal any more with this concept. That you must see.

You will come to a moment in your life when you will see that Joseph Smith has taken up so many years. Then there is a natural giving up. Then you are nothing. And this nothing is your fullness. And this nothing is all your intelligence. Then your real personality, which is no longer personal, comes up.

It is something tremendous.

If all there is is consciousness....

You spend tremendous energy living in becoming; tremendous energy is wasted in the becoming process.

See it very clearly. You see it. You are released from it.

What is the forefeeling?

When there is inquiring...it is through inquiring that understanding comes. In this understanding the mind is different, becomes orchestrated another way. It is a mind which is more essential. It is no longer a disturbed mind. When the mind is no longer disturbed, when the mind becomes oriented, then there are gaps which are not an absence of activity. Rather you have the impression that these gaps are like windows where reality comes in. That we can name forefeeling.

This forefeeling is a kind of admiration. This admiring comes directly from what you admire. When you are not taking yourself for an admirer you will become what you admire.

In the forefeeling is the substance that comes really from what you admire. When you are completely attuned to the admiring, it brings you to the threshold of the admired. It can bring you only to the threshold. It is still a process of subject-object relationship. It is a gate. From this threshold you are taken. Nobody takes you. It is a sudden insight. It is a total absence of yourself. Because this presence can only have its own place in your absence. As long as you believe you are somebody there is no place for this presence.

All your patterns will change. It will even be an effort to try and find yourself in this pattern. You will understand that there is no pattern, that every moment in life is new.

It seems that when we stop discriminating the heart opens to everyone, there is just love. In that situation what happens to love with a spouse? What would be special about two people if there is no specialness?

What you call specialness is a characteristic which you have detected in relation with the other person and you have superimposed it on the other person. So you don't really see the other person. You see only the superimposition.

What brings people together is this love. You can be sure that when there is no yeast in the cake there is no cake. It is only in this love that the real characteristics come up. Only when you feel yourself in this love can you see it in another. And this love can make the other completely free. Otherwise, if you see yourself as a woman you have only a relationship between woman and man, or with son or daughter. Then there is repetition; when there is superimposition there is repetition. But when there is a real love relationship there is not a fixed personality, and then the people around you are very rich. It is when you are looking for security as a woman that you super-impose clichés, certain ideas, certain patterns on the other one.

But what would cause you to stay with one particular person?

Go back in your life to when you were young and you met somebody and you said this person is really perfect, I love this person. Ask yourself what has given you this love. It is because this person has given you freedom, has not fixed you in a pattern. There is no memory. It is beautiful.

Meet somebody and don't superimpose your memory on them and you will see that so much richness comes out. Otherwise you superimpose, you project a cliché, and you imprison the person. You react according to the pattern you superimpose. This you must see. It is very interesting. When you live with a woman or a man and you see them every day, there is a kind of repetition. But when there is no you and he or she, no you and your son, or you and your daughter, there is a current of love, of friendship. This love which is freedom from memory, is the yeast that you really need. Even the relationship that plays such an important role, the sexual relationship, becomes healthy and permanent only in this freedom from memory. Otherwise, it becomes boring.

I am sure you feel that this is right. Then when you're seventy-six and there are not many things left to say to your husband you will find richness in silence.

August 2

How can I learn to really relax?

When you direct your attention to a part of the body, there is
a slight reaction. So I would say do not direct your attention
to the part where there is heaviness or resistance, direct your
attention to a part which is completely relaxed, transparent,
and from there invade the unhealthy part, until you have the
whole feeling of your light body.

You can contact your body on so many levels, but even
the body in a completely healthy state appears in you, in your
consciousness, your attention, in your listening, in your
awareness. All these words are the same. When you really
listen to your body, it is an object of your observation. When
your observation is like that of a scientist, without anticipation, only inquiring, then you will feel a space-sensation
between yourself and the observed. You will further feel
yourself observing. Then there is a moment when the observed vanishes completely in the observing so that there is
no observed nor observer. You can never fix, never localize
the observing because it is beyond space and time.

In this observing is the total absence of yourself. It is your
real presence.

Inside there is a voice that constantly talks—endlessly chatters—

and I am wondering what that voice is and who it is talking to.

You are aware of it, otherwise you could not know it. First, become familiar with this coming and going, accept it. You will see that you don't accept this coming and going. You don't go with it, you fight, interpret, refuse. In all these reactions you feed the comings and goings. You give them fuel. When you do not feed them you will see that these upcomings will no longer be maintained because very often they are residues from postponed ideas. But when they come, don't try to analyze or in any way emphasize the upcoming. You are the knower, so emphasize the listening, the awareness.

Listen to your surroundings and make acquaintance with listening itself. Your attention must be bipolar—listening without projection, without going in any direction. Only be open, receptive. Receptivity belongs to your whole body.

In dual teachings the notion of service has an important role but in non-dual teaching the idea of being of service doesn't have much meaning. For me, wanting to be of service is a strong desire and leads to attachment to the idea of being a server. Could you say something about the transition to action without a sense of doership?

When you live in this society and some elements of the society ask you for help, if you see you are able to help, help—but don't try to be a professional helper. Ask the question, "What is my motive for helping?" Perhaps it is a compensation, a going away from yourself, a looking away from the essential. The most useful help for society is that you are free from help yourself. But when the moment asks for help, help!

You spoke this morning of body-music and body-vibration. My experience is that there is one energy, but in this there's a scale of energy beginning with the gross, carnal bodily sensation that has many distillations and moving to feeling and the subtle body vibration or music. When you speak of the integration of energies, are you speaking of the integration of all these manifestations?

First you must face the body as it appears in the moment itself. Let the body speak as it appears in the moment itself. You will first contact the surface of the body, the outer layer. When the outer layer is completely expressed you will come to deeper levels because there is a big palette of feeling in the body. You will come to the level where there is only vibration. This vibration is like music. When these vibrations expand—because the nature of the vibration is expansion—then you come to the moment of a very big expansion where there is only vibration. And in this complex of vibration you will find one moment what we call the *nada*, original sound, from which all sound, all vibration, comes. These are still all objects. But I would say these objects tend to be integrated in your presence, in your observation, so you must not be fixed on the vibration. In any case you cannot hear this music if you are not ready to hear it. It can never sound for profane people, only those who are oriented.

Every organ in our body has a certain vibration and when you take all the organs together there is a very great harmony. It is certain that in a new age of therapy we will use sounds. When an organ does not function it means it is out of tune. Certain organs in the body belong to the sound itself but others belong to the harmonics; the harmonics are very subtle. These organs are very delicate and can come out of tune very quickly.

Sounds have not only an effect on the physical plane but also on the emotional plane. Sounds and colors have not only a physical power but also a psychological power. When we say "blue," on the physiological level it is a cool color, calming.

From the point of view of the painter, blue gives perspective, and from the psychological view there is adoration in the color blue. So colors too have a big effect on many levels and play an important role in healing through visualization.

But one must not be systematic. There are people who heal through sounds. They say we have seven cervical vertebrae which belong to the seven sounds, and we have twelve dorsal vertebrae which belong to the half-sounds. It is a little too easy. [laughter]. It is a very artificial way of thinking.

Another question comes up from what you're saying regarding the energy body. In some texts it speaks of there being five different manifestations of the body, the physical, energy, emotional, mental and divine bodies. I assume that when it says emotional body it doesn't mean the emotive body. Can you talk more about how we can work with these other bodies?

I never face any *particular* energy. What you are talking about belongs to the progressive way and you know I do not practice or advocate the progressive way. When I went in the direct way I didn't have much time to lose myself in progression!

Can I interrupt for a minute—what I spoke of is from the Crest Jewel of Discrimination *by Shankara, which is an Advaita text.*

But although he named it, he never worked on it. He points directly to the ultimate and from the ultimate he was waiting for the transforming in space and time of the parts of the body. I am not interested in all these fractions.

Become more and more acquainted with your body on all its subtle levels, the fine vibrations which are really music, because when we talk of things created, they are only vibrations, nothing else, energy in movement and matter. In poetic language we can say the world is created by music. As we are the world, the universe, all the music of the universe is in our body.

Something new has been happening to me in this seminar. I realize I have spent many years cultivating this "I" and even on my spiritual path, cultivating certain states of awareness and trying to become more present in my life in general. And I'm coming to a point in the last few days where I'm really beginning to see what seems to be the essence of what you're saying, that this "I" that I have been cultivating all my life is an illusion. That is beginning to dawn on me for the first time. It has always been there and I've always resisted it out of fear, but now I'm seeing it. I noticed today that there was a lot of sadness around that and I wondered what you have to say about all this.

I think, go home and see your life from an undivided mind, a choiceless mind free from selection. In seeing your life so, what you see will bring you certain understanding, certain conclusions. In seeing your surroundings so, you will find yourself out of the becoming process. You will do things that have to be done but you will not become the doer. At the end you will come to the deep intimacy with yourself, the absolute autonomy. You have, in a certain way, understood that the existence of the person is an illusion, a fabrication from memory, looking constantly for security. So the moment you become free from the person you no longer deal with this reflex and you will live completely in the absence of yourself and you will become a happy man.

But do not give anything up intentionally. Do not organize anything with intention. When you really understand your life, even your practical life, financial, etc., you will do it in a completely different way. But as long as you are on this earth you must earn your livelihood to live. It is not a problem to live. It only becomes a problem when you live in the becoming

163

process. Then you spend enormous energy and work every day for being unhappy!

Is there any relationship between spontaneously awakened kundalini and the realization that we are not the person? Is this irrelevant or is there some correlation?

When there is understanding, when all is understood, automatically the energy centers, what they call chakras, awaken. The understanding of the truth is also the awakening of our subtle energy. So, to focus and work on the awakening of kundalini has no meaning. It is a completely artificial procedure which takes you into the progressive path of subject-object, seeking experiences and forgetting your true nature. If the research of kundalini is for healing, for medical purposes, that is completely different I agree, but for spiritual awakening—no!

I remember twenty-five years ago I met some important people in India. It was just before the invasion of Tibet by China. I met some Tibetans who had a high function in certain Tibetan centers and we became very friendly in a very short time. They told me that some of their monks would be coming to Europe and they asked whether they could have my address. I gave them my address. They told me that these monks had realized absolute freedom, that they were really free. I said to them it is marvellous that you send such friends to me. So the monks came to Paris and I showed them all the sights and we went to the wide avenue that goes to the Opera and, as you may know, there are many picture houses and theatres. I see it all again clearly! I observed these men at several different moments and the most noticeable thing was that their sexuality was not at all integrated in them. They were completely disturbed by all the beautiful women who passed us. It was so striking for me that when we passed a picture house with posters of women almost undressed they were completely disturbed! So I thought, these people who are completely free are not absolutely free.

To come back to your question, there is no meaning in opening certain centers without being really free. It is completely a waste of time and energy. This does not mean you don't look at a beautiful woman or a handsome man when you are free! It depends *how* you look! [laughter]

August 3

Yesterday afternoon I think you said that psychological acceptance is when there is somebody there accepting, and real acceptance is just the accepting and it doesn't matter what you accept, there's just accepting.

Yes.

What puzzles me is that it seems that in order to really accept one would have had to have gotten rid of the ego and you don't get rid of the ego till you know who you really are. It seems like a paradox, because in order to know who you are you have to accept. Can you explain this?

To know something about your finger you must accept your finger. You must know something about the shape, the joints, the temperature. Accepting means with a view to know. It is more or less a scientific approach. It is an unconditioned acceptance that has nothing to do with fatalism. Just unconditioned acceptance with a view to know. In this acceptance there is no place for anybody, only acceptance. You cannot localize this acceptance anywhere, not in your body nor in your mind. It is openness; it is your nothingness. It is completely unfurnished.

Is it the same as when you say welcoming?

Exactly the same. In this acceptance nobody accepts, there is only accepting. When you accept something there's a moment when you are no longer bound to what you accept. When there's an "I," there is psychological acceptance and you are bound to what you accept. In your totality you are not bound to the object, not bound to the situation. Then you will see what happens. You will have the experience of space between you and what you accept because you are no longer stuck to it, no longer identified with it. This acceptance is your totality, your wholeness. It is not divided into positive and negative, like and dislike. Dislike and like belong to the divided mind. In reality they do not exist, they are not needed because the solution is in the situation, the action is in the situation. Every situation has its own action. So the situation acts through you, but there is nobody who acts.

So come to the moment where you feel space in what you accept, and as what you accept is in the acceptance, as the accepted has its potentiality in acceptance you will feel that the accepting refers to itself, that openness refers to its own openness. It *is*, it is your total nature. Do you see the difference?

Yes. I see clearer now.

Psychological acceptance is not acceptance. The ego accepts what gives it pleasure and what doesn't give pleasure it pushes away. So the ego identifies itself with whatever gives it pleasure and this identification automatically brings suffering. But you must experience it in the moment itself. When you have problems in your life, you will see that when you accept them psychologically that you are tormented. There is enormous suffering. The moment you accept them in your totality, you will see that the point of view of the ego is only a fraction. It is this fractional view that brings suffering. When you see things from your wholeness, your globality, you will see many elements in the situation which you didn't see before. You'll see new things in your life that were concealed by your fractional looking. A fraction can only see a fraction and action that comes out of fractional seeing is fractional. And what does fractional mean? It means not integrated in your wholeness, lacking in harmony.

So choices made from the ego will always bring suffering because you cannot have pleasure without its counterpart, pain.

What about making long range plans? I find myself wanting to make plans for far into the future. It is hard to do this without taking myself as an object, but it seems some long range plans are necessary if things are going to take place. How can I do it without objectifying?

When there is object-to-object relationship there is choice and you know the person and its needs with which you identify. It is a big cake you have cooked all your life—education, parents, society. It is very heavy to carry this kind of personality. I don't have the muscles to carry this much weight!

Then without this baggage one lives from moment to moment without making plans?

Yes, you live from moment to moment and sometimes the moment asks for action. But then you don't act any more with luggage.

I want to continue the question of acceptance. Sometimes something happens and I welcome it, but a fractional part of me says,

"No I'm not going to accept this." So what I've been doing is welcoming the saying "No," too. Is this right?

When you live in openness or you face certain elements in your life, in this openness you will have an instantaneous response and this instantaneous response is put in question by the ego. When it doesn't please the ego you push it away and when it pleases the ego you identify with it. But you have very often had the experience of instantaneously seeing the facts, the truth, before the mind disputes it. Only after, you put it in question. You must see this in the moment itself, not later through memory.

Sometimes you will see the situation from the split mind, but there is also a part of you open to the whole and the next day you come to a completely different conclusion.

Let's say I speak to my father and I don't like the way he's living his life. I tell myself it's important to accept him the way he is, but there's a tightness inside me that refuses to accept his life.

But the moment you accept your father's life you will be open to the past. He is the result of society, education, conditioning, too.

But what happens when I don't get there? I know it, but there is an irrational part of me that says "No, I want him this way." This part does not go away.

When you accept your father you will see his life becomes open. It's not simply an intellectual justification of his behavior to say he is the result of the education of his father and grandfather and the society in 1850. What is important is that when you accept him, you will find the way to deal with him. In the way of dealing with him you will help him. He will understand himself through you, through your approach.

But you must love your father. There's no question about it, you must love your father. He has undertaken so much suffering to bring you up. There were lovely moments. He prepared you to become a man. He has done so much for you. You must love him.

[long pause]

No—it's not true? [laughter]

[Another questioner] How can I love my father? I cannot remember any lovely moments with him. He did nothing to prepare me as a woman. In fact I cannot remember any time when he was not drunk or angry.

As a child is the result of his environment, so your father is also conditioned. What you call your father is only a concept, seen from the point of view of taking yourself for a daughter. "Father" and "daughter" are concepts and from these mental images there can be no meeting. You can only free him from his problem when you knowingly take the stand of love. That means be in your total absence of being anybody, especially a daughter.

You have been talking about bringing spaciousness, emptiness, into one's life. I'm having a hard time differentiating between concept and percept. Sometimes I feel I'm experiencing emptiness in the body, but the image is so strong I feel it must be an intellectual concept, and I'm confused about this.

Once you have understood that the ego, the personality, is a mind construction which you know, that it is an object like any other object, you will no longer go into the reflex to identify yourself with this personality.

When you feel the emptiness, when you see it, you are in

your emptiness. It is enough to just see when the "I," the mind, comes in the picture. Because the I-image is an object like any other. It is a reflex, a tic. People take themselves very often for a tic. [laughter]

The I-concept stimulates in you an affect and a percept, affectivity and sensation. The I-image, the image of suffering, the happy image, all have a very strong impact. When you say chair, railway station, car or ear, there is no power in it. But when you speak of fear or anxiety, it is very powerful. When you pronounce "fear" you already tremble. The I-image has the same power.

In doing yoga in the morning this week I have become very aware of the cage of my musculature. You have said that you can see the cage but there is no prisoner. I am just becoming more and more aware of the cage. I'm wondering if it is enough to just become aware of the cage?

Absolutely. The moment you are aware of the cage, you find yourself outside the cage.

I have the first part. [laughter] I feel the cage.

Yes. You know the feeling of the cage. So inquire now who is the knower? What is the knowing faculty?

I keep on looking for something beyond the cage.

It is the object which brings you back to your listening, to your hearing. You think the cage appears as a continuity but in reality the cage is a discontinuity. The cage *lives* in continuity; it itself is discontinuity. It is an idea, but you, the seeing, are not an idea.

You find yourself in a lack of freedom, in anxiety, anger

and so on, and it is normal that you desire to get out. So you try by all means to escape. But a moment comes when you see that *you* belong to the cage, and consequently that all your doings also belong to the cage. This moment is very important. When you see it there is a stop. Then the question "Who am I?" is completely appropriate.

It is the seen which automatically brings you back to the seeing. Because the seen has its relative reality, all its substance, its reason to be, in the seeing.

Is the connection between the seen and the seeing a logical one?

When the mind comes in, yes. But when your seeing is free from the mind, free from expectation, then the mind doesn't come in, there's immediately a direct seeing. So the seen unfolds and refers back to the seeing. You can never take or grasp the seeing. An eye can never see its seeing. You can only *be* the seeing.

That the seen brings you back to the seeing is a pedagogical approach, and a very good one!

In the state or non-state of union, what is the place of drawing energy from the source, for example, in prayer, asking for something. Maybe somebody in your family is ill and you want to get some healing energy to that person. The automatic response is to pray to the universal source of energy, but it doesn't feel quite right when you are one with it. So how does prayer fit in? Is there a place for prayer?

Prayer is not for asking. A prayer which asks is not a prayer. You can only love the person who is ill. I think in this moment you stimulate the member of your family because the power doesn't come from outside, it's in the patient. The healer or doctor stimulates this power in the patient. He is a channel sent from the divine. He stimulates your own energy in you. There are, in our society, people who are very powerful in stimulating the energy of others. I think they have more reason to be doctors than the learned doctors. You know from your own experience that when you learned to be a doctor you were not a doctor. You become a doctor through your experience with patients. When you love somebody you give them energy.

When someone dies, how do you let them go?

In any case you die every moment. A thought appears and disappears. You die every evening before going to sleep and you are born every morning. Ask yourself in your profound intimacy: What is there before the thought appears, what is there when the thought disappears? What is there before I go to sleep and so on? You will see that there is life. Life has never been born. Life *is*.

So, as you get undressed before going to bed, in the same way when you see the moment has come for you to go, you get undressed. You take off all your qualifications. You put all your qualifications aside so that you are completely naked. Before going away you must give up completely. You can do it now—this giving up. Don't take all your qualifications, ideas and fears with you into sleep. It is beautiful when you see the moment to go has come and you have learned how, I would even say learned the technique, to give up. Dying is not a problem.

Sometimes one gives up all qualifications before going to sleep and then has a dream and one wakes up with the baggage of the dream. You talked about going from the seen to the seeing. How can one do this with the dream?

The seeing can also reveal itself in the dream. But as the sleeping dream and waking dream are exactly the same, come back from the seen to the seer in the waking dream.

When you go from the seen to the seeing, when you feel yourself in seeing, it's a liberation. In this being the seeing there is nobody, there is only life, only light. There is peace in it. There is real equanimity in it.

This morning you said to feel the energy and the vibration in the posture. More and more I feel this energy in my daily movements. It feels like continuously dropping pebbles in a pond, or a harp constantly being played.

It is energy which lives in you. It is a very fine substance. This energy has a healing quality. It is really sound. It is, of course, an object perceived. It also has its substance in the seeing, but it is nearer to the seeing than body heaviness.

But it is still dual. There is still the pebble falling.

Yes. But this sound vibration brings you near to the seeing.

There's often a sensation of heat throughout the whole body as if it's burning away the barriers.

Yes, it is a kind of purification. It is not a pattern because it belongs directly to life.

This vibration seems like a refuge for the mind that is easily distracted. The subtlety of the vibration is more subtle than the mind so that the mind seems to be able to settle there. It seems to be a home for the mind.

Yes, it is a transition to bring you to really being knowing, being listening.

Am I free?

When you are hungry you eat, when you are thirsty you drink. It is not a decision. It comes spontaneously out of the situation. It does not go through the discriminating mind.

In this actual situation, you hear me talking, an answer comes. Is everything mechanical then?

You hear the answer in your silent mind and the answer also comes from the silent mind. I hear your question in my stillness and the answer comes out of stillness. It has nothing to do with the mind.

So it isn't automatic. It's fresh and new.

Absolutely. I have not learned what I say to you.

So I'm not free, I'm only free if…

But you are free! Don't think that you are not free. Free and not free belong to the mind. You cannot speak of free without being bound. But still it is better to say free than not free. When you say "I am free," it frees, it relaxes all your energy. The real freedom of which we are speaking is beyond free and not free. The moment you don't think of freedom and bondage, what happens? You just act, you act according to the situation.

So the worry about making a decision is all part of the mind. All there is to do is watch it and the watching is the freedom.

Yes. Otherwise, it turns to the left. All that you elaborate in your mind turns to the left. You have experienced this in your life. The mind turns everything into sour milk.

[long pause]

Of course there's also sour cream. [laughter]

I'd like to know more about the breathing and today for the first time I understand what you mean about being passive on the inhalation. I see that in the past I have always had to do something to take in the air.

The body takes itself in charge in inhalation and exhalation. You don't need to direct it. It's not a process of will. But the moment you explore your breathing capacity you will see that you use only a fraction of your capacity. So in the breathing exercises you will first discover your capacity, and as you have understood that there are many parts in your body which are not sensed, which are not sensitive for you, the moment you sense these parts and direct your breathing to them, you nourish them, make them awake and localize them.

Breathing is powerful. Breathing is beautiful because inhalation and exhalation are superimpositions on the real background. The real background is your stillness, so every time an exhalation is accomplished you live in your stillness. You don't live in the absence of breathing, but you live really your stillness. Then you become aware of when the body needs the inbreathing and you immediately use all your capacity in this inhalation.

Exhalation and inhalation are pointers to what you are fundamentally. After each exhalation you feel really at home, and the inhalation comes up out of this homeground.

Breathing has a spiritual value. It is also used to give the body energy, but then it is used in another way. As we have done it till now it is more a pointer to the spiritual background.

Does this whole dilemma that we find ourselves in hinge on the idea that we take ourselves for a person?

Of course. It covers your real being. This thought moves many other thoughts because it cannot exist alone. It only exists in relation to other thoughts: "I'm angry, I'm alone, I move, I'm hungry." It belongs only to the this and that, otherwise it has no existence. It looks constantly for survival.

Is there a good way to see this?

Only to see the mechanism, that the "I" only has reality in connection with something: "I live, I eat," and so on. But when you insist on the "I" without association, you will see it is the only concept which cannot find substance for its existence, and then the I-thought becomes the ultimate because you can never think of it. When you say "I," simply "I," it is something other than "I'm hungry."

This is a positive, affirmative approach. It has value when you have really understood what you are fundamentally. Then you can say "I—I am." But as long as you have not understood the I-thought in this way, it is better to take the negative approach: "I am not, I am nothing, I am in my absence of a me." So when you realize really profoundly the moment of your total absence, you can also say "I." But then it is not an "I," not a divided "I," not separate from all the "I"s. It is consciousness.

Pedagogically it is better, therefore, to realize your absence so that you no longer deal with the I-image and feel your total freedom.

The space in which all objects appear, is this an absence?

Absolutely. That is what Meister Eckhardt meant when he

said, "Only in my absence, He is." When you are, He has no place.

Look at different painters and you will see which painters go from space to the object and which face the object immediately. The painter who goes from space, from light to the object, this object has life, has color. It is sensitive, it is sensual. When you go directly to the object it has no flavor. You must go very slowly to the object, go around it—do not even touch it.

Did you say earlier that there has to be a cage to be a person and anything the person wants is in the cage and limited?

Yes, the person has created the cage.

So when there is something that appears to be beautiful, even when it's a reflection of truth, is it still within the cage?

In this cage there may be moments when the ego, the person, is not present. Light may come into the cage from outside. But see that you create a system to come out of the cage because you feel uncomfortable, restricted and you turn in a vicious circle.

So all yogic methods are only postponing…

Yes. There comes a moment when you ask, "Is this really life, this constant striving, living in the past, constructing the future, competition and so on and so on. Is this life?" There's a moment when you ask the question, not with the mind but with more than the mind. You are really serious, really earnest about asking it. To ask this question you must be earnest, serious.

Following that question, it seems that the cage is constructed of many thoughts that you think are happiness.

It is true. Still, when a child is attracted by all the toys and games there is a moment when he forgets his mother. But he comes back to his mother. The objects of the world are so attractive to us and bring us to this forgetfulness. But there are moments in life when we come back. We come back and ask for our homeground.

August 4

After one has seen through the I-thought and it no longer has a hold, are the residues that come up in certain situations a conditioning in the body that will take time to work out? For example, you might see your mother and the old pattern might come in immediately.

Of course if you take your mother for your mother and you for her son—the relationship between mother and son or daughter is very strong because the mother sees the son as a prolongation of herself. So she superimposes "my son" on you and you go in the trap. See it in the moment itself.

It is not only the seeing but the impact of this seeing in you, how has it acted in you, that is important. Seeing *this* is the transmutation.

Let me be more specific. There's an ideal that many seekers on the path subscribe to, that after the moment of awakening one goes through life and never has a reaction again. My question is: Are there not momentary reactions but also the instant seeing of that reaction?

Yes, reaction is an object like any other. It depends on how you see your environment. You can see it from the point of view of your five senses, the body. You can see it from the point of view of the mind, the person. And you can see it from the point of view of consciousness. But you know exactly when you are completely at home in your absence.

What is present when you are absent?

Your totality.

How do you feel it?

How can you feel absence?

How can you call it absence if you don't feel it?

You cannot feel it. It is not an object. In other words you feel it without feeling it.

Like awareness?

Awareness could be called a feeling that is not bound to the senses.

When you are in love, when you love your love, you love yourself. You are nowhere. You know these moments when you love your love and are nowhere.

You want to take it in your hand, fix it and see it objectively. That is not possible. It creates a subject-object relationship.

What is there in the absence you are talking about? I mean, there has to be something because I am alive, I am not dead.

There is Life but not the expressions of life. Life is there.

When you see an object and you are completely concentrated on the object you feel this energy of concentration. Give it up and you will feel yourself behind you.

Give up the concentration?

Yes, give it up completely and you will find yourself behind you. But the object is still there. See what your relation is at this moment. You see the object and at the same time you are aware of the seeing.

But when you give it up you essentially have no relationship with it.

Then, I would say the object is in you. It is perceived by your perceiving, by the perceiver. Give up perceiving and conceiving, and what remains is your presence.

In that process does the object itself change?

Surely, because when you look at an object through conceiving, the object is memory. Try to see an object without memory the way a poet or certain scientists see it. See how it appears and disappears in our presence. Something which appears and disappears in our presence is no longer an object.

Well, is our presence something we are aware of?

I will make a little concession for you. [laughter] Awareness is aware of its own awareness. [more laughter]

Yes, but that is not much of a concession!

[Another questioner] A moment ago you said an object appears and disappears in your presence. Can you say more about this?

An object is the five senses. When cognition becomes recognition there is no more cognition because the five senses, sense perception, and thinking can never occur together. So the moment you give up the five senses there is only recognition and when you give up recognition you are one with the object.

You see a flower. First it is a flower through your five senses, then you recognize it and name it, then you qualify it. But when all this is over you are one with the flower.

When there is sense perception only certain things may appear. You see the flower and much more. When you let the flower become totally free, you may see certain subtle forms, certain colors which you don't see with your usual looking. Then there is a direct perception, a pure perception without the interference of the mind.

In that pure perception is the flower still there, still an object, it has not disappeared?

Oh no, there is still an object but as the object appears in your consciousness, your presence, and disappears in your presence, it has no independent existence. Logically, what appears and disappears in something is essentially that something—in this case a no-thing, consciousness.

In pure welcoming, listening, where there is no recognition, no refusal of recognition and no analysis, the object disappears as an object. What seems to be in its place is oneness expressing itself without any sense of division.

When there is pure perception there is wonder.

There is wonder, but in this oneness there is only expression of oneness.

When you are in wonder there is nobody. There is only wonder. Then the Self admires the Self.

The Self is everywhere, not localized.

Wonder is a non-state but your whole body is affected by the wonder. There are echoes of the wonder in you but you should not objectify these residues because if you do, you create a state of them, fix them. Astonishment is the same.

I'm still stuck on what you mean by object. If I'm looking at the flower...

Let us not go too quickly. When you look at the flower do you see a flower?

If I don't name it...?

Do you see a flower? No, there is only seeing. *Then* you name it and say, "I see a flower." And then you say, "I, Paul, John, saw the flower." You cannot ever have them altogether.

There is only seeing.

In the pure seeing there's presence...?

You live your own presence. There is only seeing. That you saw *something* comes after. That *you* saw it comes even later. These are only concepts.

So the appearance of the object is this coming after, me making it into an object, and the disappearance of the object is the disappearing back into just seeing?

Absolutely. So really there is no object at all.

So you're saying objects exist only when there's a subject, a personal "I" observing, and when there's no subject there's no object, just the suchness of things.

Exactly. Only suchness.

Is this why we do the yoga? To experience ourselves from moment to moment in the pure state?

I would say you live in an inquiring state. Your body is perceived but you are the perceiving. Your body is an object like any other.

If one sees things from the right brain, the artist's view, is that a time when one would be more open to inquiry?

In pure perception you are one with the perception and the perception is real. The conception is more or less a gentlemen's agreement.

So at the moment when you drop the concept and live in the percept, is this the moment to ask "Who am I?"

Our brain, our education, is built up so that when we see an object we name it. This belongs to our education, our culture. But to qualify it is something else again. It belongs to our personality, what we take ourselves to be.

In the state where the mind is not interfering, as when there is painting without a painter, is this the same open state in which one would inquire into one's real nature? Are there moments when our brain is more conducive to self-inquiry?

When there is only painting without ideas, anticipation or

goal, you are a channel for all your expression. It is in waiting that the expression takes place. In painting you are not aware of your opening. But one day you may become aware of this waiting, this openness free from somebody. This, then, is the same state as inquiring.

There are moments in daily life when you are completely free from all volition and the brain comes to its natural, relaxed, alert alpha state. Only in these moments comes the insight of what you are, but you later objectify it.

I find this moment of sudden insight becoming like the Holy Grail. It recedes. Is it useful for us to think like this, of a before and an after? Having this insight has become an obstacle for me.

I agree that *having* an insight is not good English. Rather, you are it where there is no possessor of it. Live with this being, live in the state of not knowing like a child. In knowing there is no room for the new, or an insight.

You can never objectify an insight. It is an instant apperception of reality that does not go through the mind. So when you have it, go away from it.

It must be really understood that you can never assert an insight. You cannot say, "It is this or that." In a real insight you are openness, like an open flower, no more or less.

Is it possible we've had it without knowing it?

When you have an insight there remains a certain memory. Of course this memory is in space and time. It belongs to the mind. But when you really live with this residue of the insight, I would say you are open to a new insight.

An insight is sacred. As soon as the mind touches it there is profanity.

What can you say to that person who feels that that insight remains out of reach? They may say: "I've been listening to you for fifteen years, doing what you say, and I'm still not convinced I've had this insight?"

I would say that he had a wrong approach to himself and to the world.

When someone says to you, "You are really yourself in the absence of yourself," what happens then? You stop. But you are so accustomed to dealing with objects that you try to make this stop, this absence, objective, to make "an experience" of it. We are so accustomed to subject-object understanding that we objectify the understanding by saying "I understood." When the non-understanding is completely dissolved there is nothing left to understand. There is only beingness, and we must live this beingness, this absence, knowingly.

It takes time, it takes a long time to come to the maturity, to the understanding, that we are ourselves in openness. Then there is nothing to assert or confirm. We are simply open and this openness refers to itself. One knows oneself in this openness, not knowing, like you see this chair. It is a constant wonderment, a constant astonishment.

Often you've used the word "earnest" for the truth-seeker. Is it not wondrous to you to see someone sit for twenty, thirty, forty years and never seem to come to this maturity? [laughter] How can we understand what exactly is meant by "earnest" on a path where any effort is against the self-inquiry and where making an effort of any kind keeps one in immaturity?

When you are not earnest you cheat yourself. What does it mean to be earnest?

But if we are in such bondage that we can't see this, where to begin? When you read the scriptures they almost invariably speak about the qualities of the student, personal honesty being one, and the moral virtues. It seems today that we don't hear any teachers speaking about this and yet it is fundamental.

I think that there appears in the life of every human being one moment when the question "What is life?" comes up. When you really look at this you see that you are constantly in the becoming process, never in the now. You are constantly past-future, past-future. You prepare the future with the past. When you take note of this, you are brought to ask "Who am I? What is life?" As long as the student doesn't come to this point he is not a student.

The moment the student asks the question and has no reference to the past, he finds himself spontaneously in a state of not-knowing. In this not-knowing he is in a new dimension. It isn't even a new dimension because in this, there is not any direction. One must live with the question. By living with the question I mean not looking for a conclusion, an answer, because the living with the question is itself the answer. But we look constantly for an answer.

If everybody in the world was in this state of oneness and suchness, would there be any need for existence, for life?

There would only be dancing.

I thought you would say that. So actually our essential nature is that and this is a gift from nature to us to have fun and play.

As a child plays.

Is the reason for taking good care of the body simply so that you can play with it?

189

Of course.

Is work play?

Yes. Working is playing, but we put too much weight on the word "work."

You have really gone to the core of the whole thing!

He's been pushed. [laughter]

We were speaking of earnestness. Is earnestness when you no longer think that happiness lies in a certain person or object?

By earnest we mean seeing facts as they are without controlling them, without interfering with them. Being earnest is seeing facts. You can only see facts from the undivided mind. When the mind is split in pain and pleasure, positive and negative, one cannot say it is an earnest way of looking at things.

When you are in this state or non-state, does it eliminate the need for a psyche?

There is no more psychic living. You simply function.

Is there any difference between the perception of an object from the standpoint of the relative and the ultimate subject?

This relative subject is an object like any other, but in reality there is no object.

You cannot see the relative subject and its object at the same moment because the relative subject is an object too. You must see that consciousness and its object are one. There can never be two. You think you have two thoughts at the same moment because it happens very quickly, but you don't. Awareness, consciousness, is always one with its object.

So we move back and forth very quickly like a flashing light? That is the reality we construct?

Yes.

What is it about the fact that consciousness and its object are one that is freeing? I don't quite understand that.

You are the ultimate subject. There is no object without a subject. The ultimate subject is a continuum, constantly there. In this continuum there is no time, no space. You create time and space only when you think. They are concepts. To measure, you need time. But they do not belong to what you are fundamentally. You know only space and time, but what you are is timeless.

You identify with your thoughts, time and space, but your real nature is timeless. Time and space are expressions of the ultimate, live in it, have their reality in the ultimate.

When there is wonder or astonishment, when a desired object is attained, there are many opportunities in the day to feel your non-dual, timeless nature.

Earlier you said when the insight comes, remain open, move away from it, from experiencing it....

Yes. You can never think it. When you think of it you fix it, objectify it.

Ordinarily when the word "earnest" is used, the tendency is to think of someone actively searching through books, asking questions and so on. In reality that is the ego's search. Real earnestness comes in the application of the inquiring, for example, to look between two thoughts.

Absolutely.

So that if there is a student who is sitting for years of time and space, their whole orientation is wrong and that just has to be seen.

Yes, looking in books is the survival of the "I."

And even asking questions is dangerous because you have objectified the situation so you can only ask questions playfully, not searching for an answer but just as a mutual exchange of happiness.

Yes, and the answer should never be a fixed answer. It should be an open answer. One must never assert it. So there is only openness. In this openness there is not a student nor a teacher.

Many people who never ask questions, never play, it seems to me, and it seems that they are missing something wonderful. Isn't sitting and saying nothing a wrong tendency?

There is a moment when a student may live in not-knowing and have no question. There are also people who are in the garage for a long time—many people are in the garage.

Sometimes they have questions but there is fear to ask. And sometimes there is the feeling that the question cannot be manipulated by words. I will find my own answer. I will be my own answer.

When a question is asked, a teacher has two ways: to answer or not answer. To answer means it goes through the mind and must be dissolved in the mind. So it is best to either give no answer or give an answer that creates a new question in the questioner. There are many pedagogical tricks!

But if it is asked in a spirit of earnestness and playfulness then it seems to me there are reverberations and resonances so that one belongs to the process of creation and in this process of inviting creation you learn something. So in asking playfully one comes to much deeper levels and there can be a quickening as opposed to a slow simmering and the attitude of "I am going to do it myself," which is a dubious idea at best.

I think we must become acquainted with living in not-knowing. The real knowing is in this not-knowing. You cannot formulate it or objectify it, but you know fundamentally that you are it.

August 5

I have been searching for a long time for truth or God. When I began I was crippled by anxiety and fear. Now I feel I have an innate understanding of what truth is not, but I do not yet feel I have glimpsed what truth is.

You are looking for an experience, for God, for beauty. This means you see what you are looking for as an object. I would say: Simply inquire who is looking. When you really inquire, you will see that the looker is what you are really looking for. That is the shortest way, if one can still speak of a way.

Be clear in your mind that what you are looking for can never be an object. Because you *are* what you are looking for, so you can never see it, never comprehend it. You can only be it. Being it means you have no representation, no idea of it. You are free from all concepts. When the mind sees this it comes to a stop. You are still. All your ideas of yourself, all your qualifications must come to a stop. Then you find yourself in a kind of nakedness. You are this nakedness, free from all qualifications. So, be it really. Be completely attuned to it.

In all the time I have known you, you have never really talked about sitting meditation, about what to do when we sit with you in the evenings.

It depends what you understand by meditation. Meditation is not something to meditate on, because you can only meditate on what you know already and this is memory. When you go deeper you will see that you must discover the meditator and when you uncover the one who meditates you will see that it is only a cerebral construct. Then automatically the meditator and what he meditates on comes to a stop and there is only being. Poetically I would say there is only a current of love.

Meditation is what we are. It is constant. It is not time-bound to the morning or the evening. We sit together only for friendship, to be together, or to be for a while in a laboratory to discover that there is nothing to meditate on and no meditator.

So really it is no different than being in openness at any time of day?

Absolutely. Being in openness, in non-assertion means being in meditation. It is the light behind all perceptions. It is present in your activities and your non-activities. We are it fundamentally and we can never objectify, never represent what we are fundamentally.

In other words, it is absolutely our absence. In our total absence there is presence. It is a global feeling without feeling it. But our tendency is to make an object of it.

In the progressive way we become even more conditioned because the progressive way is through subject-object relationship. The less can never understand the more. We go directly to the more and from the more we go down to the less, or, let us say, from the whole to the fraction.

In looking for it you must see that you are what you are looking for. It is an enormous discovery to see that the looker is what is looked for. So it is a total openness, a total expansion. In the beginning it may be simply attention which is still a brain function. But the moment this attention is sustained because it interests us, then we will see that the attention grows; it becomes alertness, alertness becomes intelligence, intelligence becomes awareness. So all that belongs to our psychosomatic nature and is grasping, taking, attaining, comes to a stop. Not only to a stop, it comes to a state of not-knowing, a state of "I don't know" where all is open. Every cell is open. When you are open to your surroundings, an unconditioned openness, that means an openness without any expectations, wishing and so on, then this openness refers to itself. It is a non-dual experience. So we can never touch it, never see it, never hear it as we can never see our own face. It is our nearness itself.

It feels as if something's dying....

To be, you must die. The dying of the ego is not an act of volition, it is an act of understanding. The mechanism to be something may appear from time to time but you are aware of it, you do not deal with it, so when it no longer has a role to play it disappears. You feel yourself in your globality. In this non-state of completeness, there is spontaneity. There is no more intention. It is strictly function. There is no more psychological involvement.

There is then a spontaneous giving up. Nobody gives up. When you see the false as false there is a normal, spontaneous giving up. It is in the nature of seeing something false.

I have a three-and-a-half-year old son and when I look at him from my wholeness I see this lovely little being with shining eyes who has come into my life to teach me, to be my friend, and for me to look after him while he is so little. Does he have to go through his own process of forgetting who he is and identifying with his body, mind and senses? No matter how clear I may be, he has to go through that and then eventually come back to himself. Is this true?

It is in the temporal nature of the human being to identify himself with what he is not. But as a father you must show him what he is through your own presence, your own way of seeing and living with things. You must never assert in this relation. All must be open. He has to come naturally to this inquiring. And, as you said, it is the relationship of friends, not of father to son, son to father, which is restricted living. In real friendship there is no restriction because you have no image to superimpose on your son and when you do not superimpose an image on your son, he will feel himself in this freedom, free from conditioning.

A child is the result of his environment. But you know what we mean, so you will spontaneously have this *comportement*, this way of living naturally and true.

I have some kind of understanding of what you are saying, but I feel myself still in the cage. When you talk of not taking oneself for an object or the personality, I can understand that in an intellectual sort of way and in a practical sort of way in my life where I feel it is a restriction. But when you speak of being this understanding I feel a lack. Is there any way to come to this being the understanding?

When we speak of being understanding it means a timeless moment where nothing is understood. It means silence. The moment you say "I have understood," you have objectified the understanding. This is normal for the scientist; but the scientist, like the truth-seeker, has a timeless moment before he says "I understood." In this moment before he objectifies the understanding he is in the timeless state. What is normal for the scientist has nothing to do with the truth-seeker. The difference is that the one objectifies his understanding and the other has been told that he cannot objectify what he is, so he loses himself in that timeless moment. When he has heard that there is nothing to understand, to objectify or represent, he will not be tempted to do it.

What do you mean by "loses himself in the timeless moment"?

He is one with the understanding.
When the non-understanding comes to the understanding it is like a magnet. It absorbs the non-understanding.

Is it just a habit to objectify?

Yes. But the scientist is looking for an object and so manipulates the objective world, but the truth-seeker knows that he can never be an object.
You have the experience, you know moments when you are nowhere but you are present.

Can this living understanding be prevalent in one's life?

You will discover this being understanding in many moments in daily life. Before an intention appears. Before a thought appears and when it has vanished. Or when the thought process comes to an end and the mind knows its helplessness, its limits. The mind must know its limits. When the mind knows its limits there is a giving-up.

This non-state you are speaking of, is it like the best moments in your life? I am thinking of moments with my children when there is love and wonder and joy.

Yes, but wonder and joy cannot be thought. It is an ultimate feeling. You cannot think of joy or peace. We have tens of thousands of years of humanity and language and we have not found the word that brings us beyond the words peace, love, freedom. How can you objectify freedom? It is inconceivable.

In this state of you not being there and me not being there, do I create you and you create me for the sake of playing?

I do not need to create you because I *am* you! [laughter] You are looking for fishing. You look for a fish! [laughter]

Yes!

But you will find that you cannot hook a fish.

What then do I play with?

Nothing.

I thought you would say I play with love, joy or openness.

No. Joy, love, plays with itself. Openness plays with itself.

That's because it is me.

Who is this "me"? It is a thought. Do not objectify the joy in "me." In the absence of you there is only joy. Then there is not you and me, not you and others. There is only isness.

But one of the obstacles we have is that we take it all too seriously. It is really not that serious, or do you think it is serious? I think it is a big joke, what we think we are.

Yes, it's a big joke. It depends how you see it. You can laugh or you can be still and look again.

[long pause]

In your observation there are certainly residues of volition.

Is there any way of cultivating the earnestness you spoke of? I find that at moments I am very earnest, but on the whole I take myself to be something and...

Then you are no longer earnest. Earnest means not taking yourself for what you are not. Only then are you earnest.

But I generally cannot see my way out of it. I am trying to do something. How can I get out of that trap? The desire is to be free, but somehow I cannot find the right direction. It is a combination of being too lazy and forgetting the direction.

To see very clearly that you take yourself for what you are not, is very striking. Feel the impact that comes when you see it. It must be felt in the moment of the seeing, not later through memory. See it. The shock, the impact in the seeing, is the transforming factor bringing the transmutation of your whole nature. It is not just taking note.

At periods through the day today I felt that I had left my homeground. But underneath that is the feeling that you do not ever really leave the homeground, that I just think I leave it.

When the seen points to the seeing, live the seeing. That is your homeground. When the seen points to the seeing, there is no one who sees and nothing is seen. There is only seeing. This seeing can never be objectified because you are it. It is your homeground. So every object can bring you back to your real nature. So when we ask for the reason for the existence of an object, it is only to reveal this homeground, the ultimate subject.

As we have said very often there are certain objects which, par excellence, bring us back to our homeground automatically. Beauty, for example. But every object has the faculty to bring you back to the seeing, to your real nature, if you let it.

In the same way, the heard brings you back to hearing and you cannot objectify the hearing. You are the hearing. There is no one who hears and nothing heard. There is only hearing.

This is very practical, pedagogical advice for you. Very often in daily life let go of the object and you will see that it comes back spontaneously because every object desires to come back to its homeground. But you fix it, you make a concept of it, you refuse to let it come back to you and then it dies.

August 6

It is important that you become more and more aware of your body, aware of what you are not. So you must explore what you are not. In the exploring situation you are detached from what you explore, there is space between the exploration and what is explored.

You will come to the absolutely relaxed body. This is not a passive body, but is an energetic, dynamic, elastic body. This exploration can take place in all your daily activities, so that you don't go back in the old pattern of defense, tension.

When you have this relationship with your sensitive body you will have this relationship with other levels of your body. You will find yourself out of the process, autonomous, free from your body-image. The moment you look at the body, you are free from it. But you must first learn how to look without any end-gaining.

There are many opportunities in the day to bring back the perception to the perceiving where there's not a perception and not a perceiver. It is the inner, deep stillness where nobody is still and nothing is still. There's only stillness. There are moments when it comes to you because it looks for you. Or in other words, it looks for itself because there are not two. It solicits itself by itself.

You will also become more and more free from the self-image once you have seen that it has no existence, that it is completely built of memory. You will use it less and less and, as in the end it has no more role to play, it will disappear. Then you will live really in openness. In this openness *all* is open, nothing is closed. Every object comes to the openness, appears and disappears in openness, refers to the openness. Then there's spontaneous action free from reactions.

So you must be open to all the levels of your body and mind, your muscular tension, emotivity and defense. Only in this openness is transmutation possible.

I found our group very harmonious and I thank you for coming.

Mt. Madonna
April 1990

April 21

What we are looking for is our nearest. The question is the answer, because the answer was before the question. Otherwise there could never be a question. Any other answer would be only an object. We are the ultimate subject. What we profoundly are can never be an object. Understanding this immediately produces a reorchestration of energy. Looking for something, achieving something, grasping for something, living in end-gaining, becoming—all this eccentric energy comes to a stop. It is not a process of will; it is a natural giving up. In the stillness which follows, we are completely available.

Allow whatever desires to come, to come, because you can never go to it, it can only come to you. We can never go to it because there is no way to go to it and nobody to go there. It is the instantaneous awakening of our totality which is neither outside nor inside, neither introversion nor extroversion.

It is not a state because in a state you go in and you come out. It is the light, permanent light, eternal light, which is behind all perception. This openness is our real nature where there is nobody open and nothing is open. There is only openness. It can never be named, because it is without any quality. That is why it is the ultimate negative state.

We are so accustomed in our life to functioning in subject-object relationship on the level of the mind. It is mainly the personal entity which we believe we are which hinders us from being available. Speaking simply, one should be free from being somebody. In the state of openness there is no place for somebody, for an I-concept. The question "Who am I?" is the answer. There is no other answer. It is the living answer.

All that is positive is an object, but what you are fundamentally can never be an object. It is objectless, nameless and without any qualification. It is the ultimate negative state, and in its freedom, all is possible. It is ultimate creativity. The ultimate negativity is beyond positive and negative. Because what you are fundamentally is without any quality and is timeless and spaceless, it would seem perfectly clear that no technique, no system, no so-called progression can bring you to what you are fundamentally. All this is a going away from it. The ultimate understanding is an insight that you are your totality, that there is not a knower of it, that the totality is its own knowing, that it is not in subject-object relationship. Generally, we make an object of it. Most so-called meditation is in subject-object relationship.

It is through listening, through unconditioned listening free from memory, free from any expectation, that you come to this insight. You must first have the insight, a glimpse. Then live with what brought you to the threshold of this glimpse. There will be a moment when you no longer need to do all this preparation. The understanding that your real nature is never an object, never an assertion, brings you automatically to openness, to not knowing.

Knowledge of truth exists only through not knowing. This not knowing is openness, and openness is truth. Openness is not a psychological state but a way of living where there is beauty in relationship, because there is no more relationship, there is only Relation.

So live with the understanding which brought you to this glimpse. Do not touch it or manipulate it or in any way try to make it clear on the intellectual level. Do not touch it, otherwise you take all the perfume from it. As we said, you can never produce the glimpse by will. You can only remember the elements which brought you to the threshold of this glimpse. There is nobody who has a glimpse, but your whole body-mind is struck by it, and it leaves a residue in the body-mind. Live with this residue, live in innocence, without any desire to change it, provoke it or recreate it.

Can one function in day-to-day life?

Free yourself from all beliefs, from second-hand information, hearsay. Look with a new eye, free from the point of view of the I-image, then you will discover beauty. Otherwise there is only repetition. Explore without any affirmation, without any conclusion. Live in your non-concluding silence.

Do you believe in miracles, like walking on water or raising the dead?

Oh, I don't *believe* in miracles. Every moment is a miracle when you look at it with your real eye. There are no special miracles.

That's no answer. Do you believe that special powers exist?

They exist like other objects exist. What do you want to do with *siddhis* and miracles? Have nothing to do with it. I think it is a miracle that you can sit on the chair and that you have the freedom to be yourself. It is the only freedom that you have. There is no other freedom.

Are we then locked in a prison?

We are so accustomed to dealing with objects that it is

inherent in the human being to try to look at himself also as an object. You take yourself for Edward Smith and you live as Edward Smith, accumulating knowledge in the name of Edward Smith, but Edward Smith has no reality. It may take time, but one day you will see that you have been living an entity which has no reality. That moment is a very important revolution in your life. Then you will find beauty in nothingness, in being nothing. Because in this nothingness you are all. When you are nothingness you face your surroundings in their totality. When you are nothing, you are free from choice, free from selection, free from discrimination. You let life propose to you. When the psychological "I" proposes, its propositions are based not on beauty and truth, but on survival, psychological survival for the person.

There is already in you a forefeeling of this openness, where there is no center and no border. In this openness all your intelligence is at your disposal. There is fresh seeing without the interference of memory.

Come to love yourself. Not the self that you are not, but the true self that you are. Then you will not be stuck to your personality and there will be objectless relationship. That is beauty.

Is spontaneity free of what we would call negative responses? Is it always loving?

Loving has no qualities, no name. It is not an object. You can never think it. You can only be it. What is important is that you must live with it. It must come to *being* the understanding, which is a global feeling. You should live in this essence. At first, as we said already, you can only remember the sayings which brought you to the threshold of this reality, but you must become completely impregnated by the understanding and it will dissolve in a state of silence. This state of silence is the essence of understanding. It is only in this emptiness that there is presence, silent presence. It is silent presence because you are totally absent.

Real giving up is through understanding. It is a natural flow of up-giving, otherwise there is still somebody who gives up. Then you will find your hands completely empty. It is only when your hands are completely empty that you feel a fullness in your hands. In seeing things as they are, you will become more and more free from conclusion.

Is each individual in constant tension and without the tension it spontaneously reverts to the ultimate "I"?

Yes, but you can never separate an object from the subject and the subject from the object. Subject-object, cause-effect, is only on the mind level. In globality there is no subject-object because the perceived and perceiving are one.

When you live in openness you are available, free from conclusion. Then when there is conclusion that comes from the situation, it is impersonal and belongs to the moment itself.

What does it mean to love oneself?

When you look for yourself you can never find the one you are looking for. There comes a day when there is a certain maturity in you and you will see that the looker is what he is looking for. What you are looking for is peace, silence, yourself, and it can never be an object. It is a feeling. It is a jewel in your feeling. You must love the jewel. You must be it, never go away from it. The jewel is the jewel of your heart. But first you must love what you are really, then you can also love the surroundings. When you are not, then there is love. It seems very clear, no?

In a religious way of speaking it is only when you are not that God is. But when you live with the glimpse of truth you are already orchestrated. Your energy is more or less orchestrated. Follow the shadow and it brings you to its substance. When there is intelligence, there is creativity and beauty. The ultimate is beauty, beauty that can never be defined.

Let us be for a little while in silence.

April 22

Living with our question without conclusion keeps us in openness. There is a time when we are open to the question, and there is a time when we are open to the openness.

Before the yoga this morning I felt very tight and afterwards I felt very relaxed and open. The question occurs to me as to whether it's possible to experience the openness in a body that's tight. I have my own suspicions about it, but I would like to hear from you.

When the body is expanded, it is in openness. In a certain way, you have understood how to relax the body. I would say, first give up all tensions, all reactions, and then feel your body tactile. It is only through this tactility that you can expand in your surroundings, in space. From this stance, listening to sounds, listening to words is completely different. You know, as a musician, that when you play a sound, it is a vibration you produce in the first sound-box, the instrument you are using. Then there comes the second sound-box, your environment, which is the hall in which you are playing. This second sound-box brings the vibration to your ear, to your whole body. It is a completely new hearing, completely different than when you hear directly from the instrument to your ear. One must absolutely use the environment, the room, the hall.

Music, in a certain way, is a language. When you know this language, know the phrasing, know the timing, your listening is in a kind of anticipation. You listen with memory. But when your body is completely expanded, you follow the line of the music the way you follow a butterfly. So face your relaxation, and expand the body. In a body that is expanded in space, there is no reaction; there is really welcoming, receiving, receptivity. So you see, the space feeling is very important.

I have a question about faith. The open, relaxed, expanded body-mind brings us to the threshold, yet for someone who simply believes everything you say, believes in the teaching—could that faith in itself be enough to bring someone to the threshold?

When you are expanded in space, you are in a state of allowing; you allow that it comes to you. You find yourself in ultimate receiving. Then you are one with the space, completely attuned to it. There is certainly a moment when you find yourself in the allowing, in the openness. This openness is not objective, it is not asserted.

Can faith or belief take you to that openness? Even if you do not feel the openness, is faith enough to take you to the openness, even if the body is in contraction?

The teacher must be able to free you from contraction. When there is reaction you are stuck to the object and you are far from receiving. But you know how to listen to your body. The moment you listen to your body, listen to certain parts of your body, there is a natural giving-up. You may first be aware of the weight of your arm or your legs, then the feeling of the temperature may come in, and then already the different parts of the body are in expansion. For example, when you look at

214

an object that is very far away, your looking is not fixed; it is simply looking. You feel the space in you. You are the space.

It belongs to the technique of an actor to speak to an object that is quite far away, to see the object and to have a conversation with this distant object. Then the voice changes completely. So, explore this feeling of spaciousness.

I wonder if there's a choice. I go through the day, and most of it is taken up with attention to objects, getting work done. But then part of the day might be lived in what you call expanded, a feeling of...I have it now, I can hear myself talk and still see the room. It is different than if I am concentrating on what I'm talking about. Is there a choice as to whether I can be in this space or does it just happen? The point is, do I waste a day if I keep my nose to the grindstone, so to speak, to make more money? [laughter] It is hard not to be practical and get the work done and make sure somebody else is getting their work done. But that seems to detract from the expanded feeling—I think I know what the expanded feeling is. Do I earn as much money if I stay in the expanded feeling? [laughter]

Space feeling is your real nature. It is the nature of the body to feel in space. Five or six times a day feel yourself expanded in space, especially before going to sleep. One day it will become your natural state. When you need to concentrate, you do; then you automatically come back to the organic relaxed state.

If I get into an argument with my wife and can get into that spaciousness, that would be pretty good.

It is very important; otherwise, you live in reaction and reactions are closed. One reaction inspires another reaction so you live in a closed circle.

When you have to be with angry people, you must help them.

Help them? How?

Free them from anger.

How? By not reacting?

Exactly. Not reacting. The moment you do not react, it comes back to them. They are aware of it and it is a transformation for them.

Could you say, in the context of a lifetime, what is the importance of the individual quest? For example, yesterday evening I got a feeling from what you were saying that the personality is not something one should try and change before one starts, but as you follow this particular path, the personality is transformed, or falls away quite naturally.

When there is the understanding that you are not your personality, that the personality is a very useful vehicle but you should not identify yourself with it, then you are free from the personality. The moment you are free from your personality, creativity is stimulated. Because when you live identified with your personality, you live in memory, and the personality is blocked. When you are not identified with your personality it is open, free from memory and all the intelligence of the unknown comes in—creative ideas, right actions, intelligent actions.

Can you talk about how there can be differences between objects if we live in non-concluding?

In order to explore an object, a situation, you must see it from multiple points of view. When you look at it without interference, just taking it as a fact, it unfolds. When an object unfolds, it shows that you are really ready and able to receive it. Every object has its secret. It is only in your openness that the secret unfolds. But in the end the secret belongs to you. It is you who have projected the object; the object has its potentiality in you. It does not exist independently. The real personality, if we can speak of a personality, has no borders, it is not fixed. It appears only when you need it. To be really creative in space, you must be the space. I am thinking here of architecture or painting or sculpture. There must be a deep space relation, a feeling of space. It has nothing to do with thinking, conceptualization.

Is the space you're talking about now still an object?

Yes.

If it is, what is the relationship of that to consciousness?

When you are completely one with the object, one with the feeling, so that the perceiving and the perceived are completely one, then you will see that the perceived is in the perceiving, but the perceiving is not in the perceived. That makes you free, autonomous with the perceived. That is consciousness.

What is the relationship of witnessing to being one with consciousness?

Do not try to make the witness objective. When you see an object you are one with the object. Three hours later, you say you saw the object. Witnessing is not a function, because two functions do not go together. Do not make the witness objective. In any case, you are the witness. Do not create an observer, a controller.

I feel myself in space, feel mainly unfurnished, without representation, all the day. I feel it as consciousness. The eyes are open, the ears are open, but there is nothing seen, there is nothing heard. Maybe we can call it audibility or visibility, but there is nothing heard, nothing seen. But there is visibility, there is audibility. You see what I mean?

Most of the time we are identified with objects, but not consciously. Can we consciously become one with the object you are talking about?

When you see an object from the point of view of the I-image, you are identified with it, you are in bondage. When you see an object from your wholeness, your globality, you are not bound to it. See the difference, experience it in life. When there is a personal relationship with objects, there is bondage.

That is what we mean by saying an object is not independent. Would it be helpful to let the mind know that they are not independent? It seems as if we automatically think that everything is separate.

In the moment of seeing an object there is oneness. The object appears in the seeing. It is only on the level of the mind that we say there is a seer and something seen. On the level of consciousness there is only seeing. When the mind is informed of the true perspective there will be maturity.

What do you do or not do with the mind?

Live with the object, ask the question of the object, make the acquaintance of the object. Live only in questioning.

You know by experience that the moment you establish a personal relationship with your surroundings, you are bound to them. But in seeing our surroundings objectively, as facts, we are not bound. When our surroundings are free, they come to us, express themselves to us. We feel our surroundings in us, but we are not in our surroundings. It is only when our surroundings are in us and we are not in them that there is real looking, real seeing, real understanding.

How can we see something and not make it into an object?

It becomes an object the moment you name it, qualify it, judge it. An object is known through your five sense perceptions and the sixth sense of conceptualization. The body of your lover is perceived and the intelligence of your lover is conceived, but when you are free from the perceiving and the conceiving, you are one with your lover. Then there is no longer a lover and beloved. There is oneness. That you know.

An object is perceived by your five senses. An object in itself does not exist. It needs light, it needs the sun, it needs the shade and it also needs other objects. All this belongs to our sense perceptions. When you inquire into all this beauty—how light caresses an object, how light makes an object—in the end you see that an object is nothing other than light.

And what is light? That is consciousness. When you explore with your five senses, you will be astonished because it opens you to a completely new concept of reality. You discover new words. You come to a new language, a new formulation. All this exploration occurs when you are a ripe explorer. A mature explorer is free from looking for results. You can never really explore when you look for a result.

After I asked the question I remembered the Zen saying: They say that mountains are mountains and rivers are rivers. Then you come to a point when mountains are no longer mountains and rivers are no longer rivers. Ultimately mountains are just mountains and rivers are just rivers. I think that is the point you make.

Yes. First, it is a percept. Then in life somebody comes and says, "It is a percept because you perceive it" and you are for a moment one with the perceiving. This is the deep insight. Then you see that the perceived appears in the perceiving. All this belongs to a certain quality of feeling. You see a mountain, you look at a mountain, and you are the mountain. It is you, in a certain way, who project it. It is the quality of feeling. You can conceptualize, you can project many ideas, but what is important is the feeling.

Do beauty and purity have a greater power to bring us to awareness than just any mundane object?

All the beauty that you feel is the beauty of your Beloved. But any object is a pointer, pointing to the ultimate, because it has no existence in itself. It finds its existence in the perceiving, in consciousness. When you emphasize the beauty in the object, it is only a "Hallelujah!" to the ultimate.

Does this same pointer exist for emotional states?

When emotion has the character of emotivity, then it is a reaction. When it is an emotion it comes out of the ultimate itself, it comes from your heart. Emotion is not objective; it is ultimately subjective. But when there is reactivity, it is an object of your observation. You can discover in yourself whether it belongs to emotion or to emotivity. I think in our dictionary there is no distinction, but emotivity is psychological and emotion is free from the psychological.

Most of what we see is experienced in our thoughts and our feelings, in our activities and reactions. It seems to me that it is colored by this identification with myself. So the question is, where does one start? If I try to start with the object, I am doomed. Is it possible for me to work with this idea that I am only consciousness in such a way that it begins to have an influence so that I can give up all this striving and doing?

Striving and doing stop the moment you see that there is not a doer and that you can never find an answer. In striving, all you can find is an object. It is very important that you see this striving energy in you, this looking for a goal, looking for a result, looking for finality. It comes out of the insecurity in yourself, the insecurity of the I-image. The I-image is rooted in insecurity because it is not independent. It can only live in situations that you create. So you constantly create situations from memory, from the past. See it, understand it and feel the impact the seeing has on you. This brings transmutation, transformation. But you must see it in the current of life.

When you see that you are not an object, when you immediately see all that you are not, then you automatically live in consciousness. This is not a concept, it is a feeling—if we are allowed to qualify it. It is a feeling of being free, being free in fullness, in completeness, a feeling of ultimate satisfaction. One is free from all possible desire.

[long pause]

It is as if you walk in a forest, the sun is rising, and you realize in one moment that it is Sunday and that you do not have to work. [laughter]

Do you think it is possible for us, living very busy lives and subject to outside influences every day, to have this awareness?

Be free from the opposites. See how the mind fears being free from the opposites. Live in the heart. The moment you live in the heart, it refers to itself. Then there is no more qualification, there is no more mind; there's only oneness, love.

May I ask you something? When you sit there and you shut your eyes and you're quiet, are you meditating? Do you have to meditate any more? Or does it follow you, stay with you?

There is nobody. The eyes are more or less closed because the eyebrows are heavy. [laughter]

Sometimes when I am in a busy place like a grocery store at rush hour or in a big group where everybody's talking, my listening shifts, and instead of being able to hear specific words or understand anything, all I hear is a lovely babble. Is that the kind of thing you are talking about when the self evolves, and you are not listening to anything, you are just hearing?

There are moments when you hear sounds, but you can't distinguish anything. As long as you have ears, it will be so. This kind of audibility, which is not really hearing, is there. Likewise, the eyes may be open and you do not see any special object, there is nothing seen and nothing heard. But meditation, presence, is everywhere there. Very often people close their eyes or ears in a kind of introversion. This kind of introversion does not bring them to meditation. Meditation is when all is present. All that is, all that you are, is in this stillness. It is beyond the stillness of the senses, of the mind. It is behind the mind. You can have it before the body wakes up in the morning. The world is not awake because the body creates the world, but there are moments when you are lying down where there is nobody present and nothing is present, but there is presence. You will not feel it every morning, but as I have pointed it out to you, you will discover it.

On the one hand this doing, any doing, seems incompatible with the no-practice that you teach. On the other, there is the feeling that certain techniques help to clear some of the contraction. I think that many of us here are involved in psychology in one way or another, and I wondered if you would speak on that.

Psychology refers to the progressive way. Here we are concerned with the direct way. The progressive way is progression in the mind, but what we are fundamentally is not mind-stuff. It is beyond the mind. That is why we do not refer to the progressive way, but we may, in certain circumstances, use elements which belong to the progressive way. It depends how one deals with these elements. As long as you believe that there is an independent entity which can become more and more good, more and more simple, more and more honest and so on, with practice, then you are on the progressive way. The progressive way functions in subject-object.

As a psychologist you know that there are certain tensions in your patient, certain reactions, aggressiveness, and so on. You feel it, you see it; you even feel the tension in the room. Then you should have a conversation with your patient. The patient comes to you to be healed; it is only because of an uncomfortable feeling in him that he comes to you. You must question him. The moment you question him, he is obliged to give an answer. To be able to give you an answer, he must listen to himself. You ask, "Is it warm? Is it cold? Is it dense? Is it heavy?" and so on and so on. You do not need this kind of information, but in this moment you bring your patient into the situation of listening. The experience is listening. In this listening, there is a curative state. He becomes detached from his illness. As he is no longer in complicity with it, it unfolds, you can be sure. You must deal only with the present physiological state. Going back to the past, to your father and mother, crying, screaming and rolling on the floor is no solution.

Sometimes you speak of listening to the body, and sometimes you speak of seeing it or observing it. I am wondering if there are moments or circumstances when it is more appropriate to do one or the other?

To listen to the body the interfering "I" must be absent. It is the same in seeing or observing, the same presence without someone who is present, listening, seeing, looking. There is only awareness without anyone aware.

Generally we take into sleep with us all of our qualifications, what we call ourselves. When the body wakes up in the morning, all of these qualifications wake up also. So it is important to make ourselves completely naked in the evening, and in the morning try not to go into the old patterns of feeling and thinking. Be only looking or doing free from the point of view of the doer. It is the doer who makes the work difficult. When there is simply doing, you are no longer psychologically involved in it. There is only doing, there is only functioning. In reality we are only functioning. We are seeing, we are hearing, but there is not a seer, not a hearer, not a doer, not a functioner. There is no entity in the cosmos; there is no entity at all.

Thank you for coming.

April 23

You may have some interesting questions.

During meditation and the body work there is oftentimes an experiencing of a presence, and with it comes a feeling of gratitude. The first time I heard you speak I had a brief glimpse of something which felt more like a no-presence. It didn't come during a meditation or any conscious effort to still the thoughts; it was just an instantaneous flash of what felt like no-mind. So my question is: Is the experiencing of a presence, and the experiencing of non-presence the same thing? Or is one a preparation for the other?

In your case, the presence is mind; the absence of presence is consciousness, beingness. When you hear the perspective of the truth, you listen to it. It is mainly a formulation referring to what you are not—that means, body, senses and mind. This knowing belongs to the mind, is on the mental level. It is in the moment when the teacher exposes what you are not that what is appears. It is an experience without an experiencer, a glimpse of truth, an insight. But there is no presence. Nobody is present. Put another way, there is only presence, but this presence is not objective. It cannot be known by the mind.

We know ourselves mainly in subject-object relationship, but what we are fundamentally can never be an object. When you look with the wrong perspective, all that you look for is objective and all that you can find is only an object. One day you will see that this takes you nowhere and in this seeing there is a giving up. When you really live this upgiving you come, in the end, to the understanding that the questioner is the answer, that there's no objective presence. It is only in the total absence of yourself that we can speak of presence. And this presence refers to its globality. Once you have had this glimpse, this insight, then keep it. You may go away from it, but when you remember yourself and the formulation which brought you to this threshold, you will again be brought to this experience without an experiencer.

You will find yourself in openness. Openness can never be an object, because openness refers to itself. Become open to the openness. So follow the line which brought you to the threshold of your insight, the glimpse of truth. When we use the word "presence," we mean only this presence when there is a total absence of yourself. This moment is not conceptual; it is perceived, it is feeling, global feeling, not the feeling as when you feel something. It is a feeling without feeling.

You have spoken of emotion, like the feeling that one gets when looking at a sunset. How does this kind of feeling fit with the other "feeling without feeling"? There seems to be a tangible presence about the feeling of joy.

In the moment of wonderment, there is no subject-object relationship, no perceiver. You are completely attuned to beauty; there is oneness. When you adore beauty, you are in a state of adoration, where there is *only* adoration, and not a knower of it. This adoration comes from the adored. So when you follow your adoration, you will automatically find yourself in the adored, the perceived in the perceiving, because there are not two; there is only one.

You would like to see the sunset, feel yourself in wonder, and at the same moment be an observer. That's not possible.

When you say "I'm happy" you are no longer in happiness because you have objectified the oneness and put it in subject-object relationship. You have made it an experience with an experiencer. You can have many experiences, many, but all these experiences are in the realm of the mind. The real experience is the non-experience.

Sometimes I receive teachings or have glimpses in dreams, and I wondered if you would talk about those kinds of dreams and how to work with them—to bring them from the dream state into waking life, in some way integrating them.

You can have a glimpse of truth in a dream, as you can have it in the waking state. In the morning, when the body wakes up, you say, "I dreamt I found myself in fulfillment," and the residues are in your body-mind. So what you can do is to keep these residues from the non-experience. The residues may leave an organic memory which may solicit you and bring you back to the fulfillment.

May bring you back to that experience in the waking state?

Exactly.

They don't seem to have the same impact on the body-mind in the dream state as they do in the waking state.

But still they are residues, the same residues as when you come out of deep sleep. There are residues from deep sleep that you ignore, residues of peace, of beauty, of freedom.

Is it helpful to write dreams down? To bring them and their residues to the waking state so that...?

I would not write it down, because then you fix it. But I would take note of it, that is true. Also bring the perceived back to the perceiving. Let the perceived unfold and dissolve and abide in the perceiving which is a global feeling.

An object is never detached from truth, because it exists, has its homeground, its support, in truth. That means an object can never exist without truth which can be called the ultimate subject, our real nature. Every object, therefore, can bring us back to our reality.

It is important that you discover in you the eternal question. The eternal question is the answer. When you ask the eternal question you are completely open, open in not-knowing.

In human relationships, it seems that most of the conflicts we experience are interpersonal conflicts which are the result of personalities clashing. In other words, it's personal. When I listen to you and to the questioner trying to fix you at the level of the person, it seems that you refuse to get involved at that level, or you simply don't get involved. My question is: Does there come a point as we move along on the path of this teaching where it's important to actually refuse to get involved in the personal in our relationships with others?

It is the idea of being somebody which cuts you off from a global relation with your surroundings. From the point of view of the person, there is constantly choice and selection, looking for security. This, you know. On the level of the person there is no understanding, there is no love; there is relationship but there is no real relation. The moment you take yourself for "a person," you can only see other "persons" around you. Just as when you take a stand on the level of the senses a word is sense perception; and from the level of the mind, it is only a concept, but from the stand as consciousness, the word is consciousness. So in the same way, when you take a stand on the level of the mind, of the person, you can only see persons. Thus one person is in constant insecurity, looking for security in other persons. This looking for security may even be expressed in goodness, in giving, in serving, and so on. But this social behavior often comes from the need to create security for the person and rarely from real compassion, freedom from the person.

The person is only a concept, built up by experiences, hearsay, beliefs, education, language. When you really see this, then the concept gives up, gives up itself, and you find yourself free, absent from the idea to be somebody. Look around you in this freedom from selection. You will see facts, things around you, that you never saw before when your seeing was fractional, seen from the point of view of the person. It is the most important moment in daily life: to see that you are nothing. It is in this nothingness, this absence of representation to be somebody, that there is fulfillment, globality, total presence.

Is this nothingness the point of death and life?

It is only in this nothingness that there is fullness. The word "nothingness" refers to all that is objective, because all that is objective is your projection. What you are is consciousness, the ultimate subject. That is your nearest. It was already, before your parents conceived you, even before the creation of Adam. In this case the problem of dying has no meaning.

There's nobody who lives, and nobody who dies. It is important that you keep this insight. It is this insight which brings a new orientation into your life. You can never change your life. It is only from this non-point of view, of consciousness, that there is change, that there is no more compensation. In other words, you are oriented; all your dispersed energy is reorchestrated. It brings you to a new understanding of life, a new way of behavior. A new behavior cannot be obtained intentionally. It is the glimpse of reality which changes the chess board completely.

When you talk of earnestness, does it mean being attuned to that glimpse?

Yes, by earnestness I mean to live with this understanding, and to see in daily life how this understanding acts on you, how it brings you to a new orientation. That is what I mean by earnestness. There's no more dispersion.

What about effort? In other words, having had a glimpse and being aware how it acts on us, subsequently we may feel that we have strayed from that glimpse, that we are not in tune with that glimpse. Sometimes it feels like there is some effort required to find our way back.

But the effort can only come from a somebody. The effort is intentional, involving choice. When there is a glimpse of truth, the body is affected, expanded, then when you are again engaged in striving, in end-gaining, in the becoming process, you feel it in your body. The body is no longer expanded in space. There's no more space feeling, even in thinking. So you are aware of the contraction because your new organic body feeling of freedom solicits you. When you do not ignore this solicitation you become more and more free from psychological memory, past and future. You find yourself more and more in the actuality, the presence, in the now. All this has nothing to do with thinking or representation; it is an original feeling. In our language we have no word for this original feeling, this original apperception.

So when we feel ourselves inscribed in the end-gaining, should we just be aware of it?

Exactly. Yes. Be aware of it. And then you turn your head.

It's a discovery in not-doing. In really not-doing, there is doing. But there's no interference of the person. You act according to heaven.

Act according to...heaven?

Heaven, yes. [laughter]

So we let the body's space-feeling be our guide and stay attuned to that feeling and when we feel contracted, we are aware of the contraction.

This feeling of expansion, space, is your real nature, because your real nature is space. It is only your reaction, your anxiety, your fear, which brought you to contraction. When you were a child your reactions eventually became a chronic condition and now you believe you are this tension, this conditioning. But a time will come when your expanded body will become completely integrated.

What happens when one realizes one's spacious nature?

When you recognize that you react, you may not react against this reaction and you will be free of the vicious circle of reaction. The moment you are free from the reaction, look again at what produced the reaction. You can do it at any moment in daily life.

You may several times find that you are reacting, but you

will no longer react against reacting. That state will last for some time, then there's a moment when you will be aware in the moment that you are in reacting, so you will not accomplish completely the reacting. It is interrupted. The impulse is interrupted. Then you will feel it before the impulse strikes your brain. It is very interesting. [laughter] I would say then that you are completely free. People on the street can tell you that you are an idiot, and you won't react.

Where does this I-thought, the ego, come from? I can see how the I-thought builds upon itself and reinforces itself, so that it becomes a really strong ego, a contracted personality. But where did the very first impulse to identify as a separate "I" come from in the first place?

It comes from memory. What we generally call memory is only for maintaining the "I," the person. When you see really that the "I" is a concept, then you are free from psychological memory. But functional memory continues. You use it when you need it, in the moment itself. But you don't daydream any more, you don't invest your memory or project it into the future. There comes a moment when you ignore the person and in the end, you forget it.

So this "I" doesn't come from anywhere? We just imagine it.

Completely. When the body wakes up in the morning, where is the "I," the "me"? Realizing this is a moment for laughter.

I notice that I live from several points of view. Sometimes I live from the point of view of someone who needs an answer, who is trapped in a situation and needs a way out, but there is really nowhere to go. And at other times it seems as though there is just listening itself and there's no motivation behind it. That feels really clear. But I don't see where there's a choice involved in what point of view I take.

You know moments in the day when you face facts, when you don't judge them, interpret them, you simply accept them without conclusion. In these moments you are no longer stuck to the situation, you are free from it and then there is understanding of the situation. Only then is there right acting. When you look at your surroundings from the point of view of the "I," you are bound. But when you see your surroundings from your globality, you are free from them. This freedom is not a concept, it is an original feeling. Freedom is not a concept.

A couple of nights ago, you said, in response to someone's question about miracles, that the real miracle is to be sitting here in this chair.

Absolutely. The stone, the vegetable, the animal—each helps you to sit on this chair. It is so beautiful, so miraculous that you are born as a human being, and not as a snake. There's nothing foreseen in your life, there's no free will. The only freedom you have is to attain what you are fundamentally.
 [long pause]

Sometimes it seems that one creates everything in a way, and yet at the same time the world just spontaneously appears...

You are the creator. You create every moment. You project every moment.

So even when it spontaneously appears...

It is you, it is you.

Do I have any responsibilities?

As long as you believe you are somebody, there is responsibility. When you are free from the I-image, the problem of responsibility doesn't come any more in the picture, because all your doing is adequate, appropriate to the moment itself. As long as you believe you are this person, there is responsibility, and there may be karma.

We are so accustomed to localizing ourselves, in the body, in the mind, in the feeling, in the sensing, in the representation. But this freedom of which we are speaking is not outside and not inside. You can never localize this freedom. The eyes function, the arms function, the feet function, but there is not a functioner, there is not a doer, there's not an actor, there is only acting, doing. What we are fundamentally can never be localized. It is found in non-localizing. So trying to find it through introversion or extroversion is going away from it. Do not try to remember the words spoken in these meetings. Remember their scent, their flavor, and allow yourselves to be solicited by this perfume, the silence behind all words. It comes from what you most deeply seek. It, only, is the answer to your questions.

[pause]

April 24

Find yourself in a state of non-conclusion, free from assertion, because all that is concluded is an object. What you are fundamentally is not an object, can never be perceived. When you look for it you can only find something perceived, an object. Realizing this brings you back to looking without looking for anything. Then you are in astonishment. In astonishment you are where there is no object, very near your real nature.

In daily life transpose this understanding. Do not be driven to conclusions. It is the I-concept that makes conclusions. In the absence of an I-image you are completely open to your surroundings, to the world, and free from the need to conclude. Then, free from intention, you discover your spontaneous being. In living open to your surroundings without concluding or interpreting, there comes a moment when you are open to the openness. It is a feeling that you are the vastness. Understanding must absolutely dissolve in this feeling of being understanding. This understanding is a silent feeling, an absence of all representation. At first when you say "I have understood," there is a representation, but this representation dissolves in knowing. The representation belongs to knowledge and knowledge dissolves in knowing. When knowledge dissolves in knowing, there is really being the knowing. You *are* the knowing.

Generally, you never give enough time so that knowledge dissolves in knowing. First see how the knowedge acts on you. The understanding must be really clear, because only clear understanding can dissolve in knowing. When this clear understanding appears, live with it, free from manipulation of the already known. The knowledge unfolds and becomes clear understanding before dissolving. This unfolding in silence has a special taste, a special perfume. You may have this perfume now or later. It is this taste which is important to remember. All other things exist, but this perfume *is*.

Have you any questions?

Understanding comes from consciousness and then dissolves back into consciousness. Is that right?

Yes. It comes from consciousness and it refers to consciousness. They are not two, there is only one. When you look for it, it is looking for you. When you desire understanding, it is understanding which desires you.

What do you mean?

When you feel it, it comes from what you feel. There is no feeling without what you felt already being there. It is exactly like when you follow a shadow, it brings you back to its substance. When you really live with the feeling of this insight, it brings you to the felt. So when this understanding is not really deep you make an object of what has to be understood. But what you are can never be an object, can never be perceived. What is perceived is the mind.

In doing the yoga I sense that when I can let go of concepts and form and be in spaciousness, that intelligence functions as an appropriate response to the moment. It somehow feels beyond the

conceptual mind and is always appropriate to a given situation.
There is a different feeling quality about that than the conceptual
mind.

Be free from the doer, be only doing. Be free from the action,
be only acting. The doer does not exist; it is a concept.

So could we say, then, that everything that is happening is really
coming from spaciousness?

There is only happening.

In every situation where there is no conclusion from the
I-image, you are brought back to your total absence, which is,
in reality, your presence. You are free from the object part. In
real non-conclusion you are not stuck to the object, you are
free from the object.

There seems to be some fear in me, to not conclude.

But you should immediately see who is afraid. You will see
that you have established a personal relationship with a certain situation. See the situation only in openness, free from
the I-image. You will see the situation completely differently.
This is impersonal living, because in actuality there is only
living, there is not a liv-er. So when you introduce a liv-er, you
introduce a concept.

When a personal relationship is established there are
reactions. You go from one reaction to another. So, practically
speaking, immediately face your reaction. When you face your
reaction you feel yourself out of the process. This feeling is a
complete absence of yourself, absence from the I-image. You
feel your space, your vastness, your immensity. The moment
you are out of the process you are no longer stuck to the
reaction. Then see what happens to the reaction. It dissolves,

because there is no longer an accomplice to it.

You talked about the pranayama actually having an effect on the patterns of the brain. You have talked before about the breathing as a way of quieting the mind. Could you say more about that?

You know that when there is insecurity in your thinking, your breathing is completely affected. So when you do certain of the breathing exercises, you quiet your thinking. When you have an important meeting which causes deep anxiety, do this breathing. Before an artist goes on stage, he first practices this breathing, and the physiological nervous system becomes quiet.

I have a question about letting go. Must we first let go of all our old ideas before the new manifests?

Before you face a situation, completely free yourself from anticipation. Face the situation in a state of unknowing. When you face the situation with intention, then you miss the real content of the situation.

In the past months I have been thinking about the idea of solving the problems in my life, forging a certain direction as opposed to letting it unfold. That is why I have been feeling....

When you see things with a clear mind, free from intention, there is discernment about what is important and what is less important. A clear mind comes when you are open and alert, especially in your situation. Alert means being free from intention, free from the "I." Then real intelligence takes over. Do not draw any conclusion from our meetings here. Simply take it into consideration when it comes to you.
Do not try to memorize anything. When it comes to you it has

its own flavor, otherwise it remains only as formulation. What is important is the flavor. The flavor is really the being understanding.

Thank you.

Works by Jean Klein

In English:
Living Truth
Beyond Knowledge
Open to the Unknown
Transmission of the Flame
Who Am I?
I Am
The Ease of Being
Be Who You Are

In French:
Sois ce que tu es
L'ultime Réalité
La Joie sans Objet
L'insondable Silence
Qui suis-je?
A l'écoute de soi
La Conscience et le Monde
Transmettre la Lumière

In German:
Freude im Sein
Wer bin ich?

In Dutch:
Gesprekken met Jean Klein
Wie ben ik?

In Spanish:
La Escucha Creativa
Quien Soy Yo

Translations also available in Italian, French, Spanish, German, Greek, and Hebrew

Journals Edited by Jean Klein:
Listening
Etre (France)
Essere (Italy)
Ser (Spain)

Videotapes:
The Current of Love - with Lilias Folan
The Flame of Being - with Michael Toms
Love and Marriage - with Paul & Evelyn Moschetta

Audiotapes:
A Clear View - with Michael Toms (New Dimensions Radio)
The Sacred Quest - with Michael Toms (New Dimensions Radio)

For information about these publications, contact the Jean Klein Foundation, P.O. Box 2111, Santa Barbara, California, 93120 U.S.A.

Blossoms in Silence

A very special book published by the Jean Klein Foundation in 1994 is *Blossoms in Silence* by Jean Klein. Over two years in preparation, the book was produced with a hand-operated letterpress and is printed on art paper, hand-sewn and bound, with a hard cover clothed in papyrus. Its "sayings" are distillations of the truth of the "direct way" prepared by Jean Klein especially for this publication and they are accompanied by abstract black-and-white drawings. The edition is limited to 200 copies, numbered and signed by the author, and will not be available in bookstores.

Listening

The serious truth-seeker will also be interested in receiving the journal *Listening*, published twice each year by the Jean Klein Foundation.

Each issue contains:
- Articles by Jean Klein
- A classic text in the field of non-dualism
- Excerpts from talks or forthcoming books
- A section on Jean Klein's work with the body
- A question and answer section
- Jean Klein's schedule of talks and seminars in the U.S. and Europe
- An update on publications of the Foundation

Readers also receive invitations to special small talks, as well as an informal "Day of Listening" with Jean Klein some time during the year.

For more information or to make a donation, contact the Jean Klein Foundation, P.O. Box 2111, Santa Barbara, CA 93120.